IMPOSSIBLE LOVE
—OR WHY THE HEART MUST GO WRONG

Jan Bauer

ECHO POINT BOOKS & MEDIA, LLC

Cover image *Great Lovers (Mr and Miss Hembus)*,
Ernst Ludwig Kirchner

Cover design by Adrienne Nunez,
Echo Point Books & Media

ISBN: 978-1-62654-973-9

Published by Echo Point Books & Media
www.EchoPointBooks.com

Printed in the U.S.A.

This Book is Dedicated to D.J. and S.D. and to all Lovers in the Mystery of Amor

 CONTENTS

 # Acknowledgments

There are many, many people to thank for their support and contributions to this book:

The analysands in my private practice and the participants in my seminars over the years who have kept the flame burning with their quests and their questions.

The friends whose affection and support have been a lifeline always, but a veritable transfusion during the writing of this book, especially during the periods when I was totally unavailable to reciprocate. Special thanks to Tom Kelly who was there all the time, at every stage, for his leaps of faith into my unknown, his eros-filled intelligence, and his "inner kid" who never forgot the play. To Guy Corneau who went before and lit the path with his own hard-won creativity and brought back messages of hope that always arrived on the days they were most needed. To Liliane Kleiner for being such a special companion in this process, her intrepid faith in the Feminine and Myth, and contagious sense of the "tale." To old and close friends Bea Reed, Diana Beach, and Connie Steiner for their long-distance encouragement, insights, and humor. To Dennis Cordell for such early-on enthusiasm in the project and to Bonnie Kushner for never doubting.

In the actual production of the book, I would like to thank James Hillman for inspiration and for helping to make an impossible project into a possible book. Ginette Paris for her generosity in encouraging me to write, taking the time to read the first draft and sharing so many interesting pointers about writing. Judith Murray for her technical help on the final draft, her patience with detail and my demands and especially her invaluable contributions to the text as an intelligent and sensitive reader. Tony Frey for a short note a long time ago in which he wrote, "It may be impossible love. But it is still love."

Finally I wish to thank Carolyn Heilbrun. Though the subjects of her books have nothing to do with this one, her work *Writing a Woman's Life* opened the doors to speak out of.

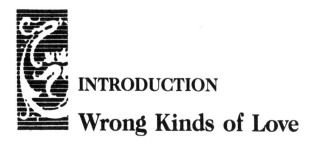

INTRODUCTION
Wrong Kinds of Love

Certain kinds of love affairs are both impossible to live and impossible to forget. They may last a month, or they may go on for years. It doesn't really matter, because they mark our lives far beyond the actual time spent in living them.

A description of these love affairs would not correspond to the relationships that psychology and the experts hold up as proof of maturity and healthy self-esteem. Indeed, they go against every official version of good and "possible" love. They happen at the wrong time, in the wrong place, and with the wrong person. They lead less to intimacy on earth than to intimations of immortality somewhere between heaven and hell. No wonder they go by the name of "impossible love," impossible to live, impossible to give up, impossible to understand—more about confusion than complicity. They exalt and they humiliate, they promise and they disappoint, but they do not bring peace of mind. In addition to all this, they usually end badly. We may become saints or sinners, but we will not become "winners" in these particular love affairs.

Frequently, we sense this from the beginning, and

we go into these relationships knowing we shouldn't. We can already count the reasons, proving it will never work. And yet we go. And once in, we stay in them long after we should, even when the impossibility is "proven" beyond a reasonable doubt. But these are not reasonable events, and they are definitely not the "right" kinds of love we would probably have if we had been reasonable in the first place and listened to the advice of concerned friends and therapists. From a healthy-minded point of view, these relationships remain both impossible and wrong.

Their impossibility may come from obvious outer taboos or hidden inner inhibitions, material difficulties or psychological differences. Whatever the cause of the obstacles that intrude between the lovers and their love, transgressing them becomes irresistible and heightens the feeling of intensity, but it doesn't make the love any more possible. It just adds to the sense of "wrongness." Wrong to love, wrong to fail to overcome the obstacles to loving.

In former times, this kind of love was called tragic, romantic, or doomed, a great passion or even a "folie à deux." Today, it is more often termed a neurosis, an addiction, or a projection. The star-crossed lovers of yesteryear have become the dysfunctional, co-dependent patients of today. In the twelfth century A.D., Abelard and Heloïse were punished and ostracized for loving wrongly. Today, they would be labeled and treated. Each epoch provides its opportunities for impossible love and creates sanctions to deal with it. Today, as in the past, in spite of psychology, people go on loving wrongly and impossibly. They may read self-help books by day, but they read love poems by night, and they feel as caught by their own contradictions as they do by the passion itself.

Why would any normal person, especially any normal person with some psychological and practical understanding, consent to such an experience? Why would anyone risk loss of control, of face, of well-being, perhaps even of family and reputation for an impossible love? Clearly, a normal person in a normal state of mind would not. Faced with the advent of passion, he or she would consider the risks and run the other way, tie him or herself to the mast, if necessary, in order not to succumb to the siren's call. And many people do run away or bravely and successfully resist before it is too late. Others, even "luckier," never even hear the song and may manage to live a whole life long without the experience of such disruptive love. It isn't for everyone, nor is it the only way for normal people to be catapulted into abnormal states. Impossible love is just one of the routes into great pain, and through it perhaps great depth and new meaning.

Death, illness, divorce, failure, reversal of fortune and hopes are a few of the other blows that life may reserve to jolt us into an awareness beyond that of everyday consciousness. Sometimes the jolt comes from outside, sometimes it comes from within. In one form or another, life provides the raw materials. Unfortunately, it doesn't give the directions or the answers. Maybe that will take a lifetime, but let us at least start by asking the questions. Not the "Why me?" or the "Who can I blame?" or the "What did I do wrong?" questions, but the *"Why now?"* and the

"*What for?*" questions. What does this event mean in my life, and how can I live it so that at my death I can say I have lived, and not that I was lived?

To ask this question takes a particular kind of courage, not necessarily of the active, heroic kind. It means holding the balance between the temptation to give up and the temptation to strike out. It means having the courage to face the "dragon" (or the symptom, or the problem, or the "bad" guy in our dreams and lives) and find out what it wants, instead of killing it and walking away untouched. It means, if we are engaged in the dragon energy of an impossible love, facing its fire and inquiring what it is bringing into our lives.

It isn't natural to do this. Even Parsifal, the hero of the Grail Quest, who went through death-defying adventures in order to find the sacred chalice, forgot to ask what the quest was all about the first time he came to the place of the grail. Because he forgot, because he just wanted to grab and run, the grail disappeared, and so he had to leave and be further tried before he could return, chastened and less greedy, to claim the prize. Like him, most of us forget many times around. We want the prizes of answers and solutions, not meaning. We may be willing to read books and pay therapists but we want results. It is so much harder to let events take their course in our lives, to meet them, and to let their meaning unfold, without over-controlling or passively submitting. When something hurts, we want to find a cause, and our "culture of impatience" leads us to look for someone or something to blame: men, women, mothers, fathers, patients, therapists, ourselves, our bodies, our lovers, our lovers' lovers.

Now, blaming is a natural reaction, and it can even be necessary as the first step in deciding not to be a victim of one's life. A good outbreak of anger and blame can be both therapeutic and empowering for someone who has accepted too much for too long a time. In our litigious society, it also happens to be much more lucrative than any search for meaning. But blaming as a way of life does not solve any problems in the long run. Rather, it cuts us off from our own power by keeping us in the role of the child and in the childlike fantasy that all in the world is black or white, good or bad, right or wrong, including ourselves. This kind of innocence can be dangerous. It leads to a fundamentalism in which absolute moral divisions create a false sense of security. It is a tempting trap to fall into when we feel confused and unsure. We all have the potential to become psychological fundamentalists when we resist coming to terms with life's ambiguities, including especially the contradictions in our own psyches.

Blaming as a way of dealing with the paradox of impossible love doesn't help, either. The love may be all wrong, but there is no right answer—no diagnosis or theory to cure it. You can blame yourself and your vulnerability or foolishness. You can blame the other's ruthlessness, seduction, and unconsciousness. Still, the love is there, inappropriate, wrong, impossible perhaps, but undeniable.

Impossible love is not just undeniable in the psyche of a particular smitten individual, however. It is also undeniable in our culture, as a myth and a cultural "imago." Whether we actually live an impossible love or not, we are all deeply influenced by the myth of the star-crossed lovers, the central image of Romantic Love. We just don't realize that behind the modern sentimentalized versions of romantic love lies the darker story, a story of impossibility, tragedy, and death, not happy endings as in Hollywood. When we think of Romeo and Juliet, Abelard and Heloïse, Tristan and Iseult, we think of their beauty and commitment, but we forget about their fate. We repress or blithely ignore their unhappy endings when we fall into fantasies of living a legendary love affair, and we are astonished by the darkness when we actually live one. As the wife of a man who left his family for such a passion says to him afterwards, "I'd like to find that certain kind of love too." And when he does not answer, she goes on to say, "But no, you're right. I doubt I ever will. It may be too cruel for me. I'd be too frightened. . . ."[1] She had seen the darker story.

And as a man said upon leaving my office after a long discussion of his discontent with a loving, but predictable partner, "Well, I guess I'm like most men I know. I didn't marry the woman I was crazy about. I married the one I felt safe with."

How lucid of him to admit this. So often we don't. We chafe in our relationships or their absence, decrying the lack of romance and/or passion. We yearn to partake in something that is more stirring, more momentous, more transcendent than the relationship we are living or have lived. We long for intensity and for transformation, but we are naive about that word

6   INTRODUCTION

"transformation." In our innocence, we often think it can just "happen" if we live right and go to the right workshops. Therapy will fix us, the workshop will change everything, or, better still, a passionate love affair will give us back our taste for life and transform our whole being. Unfortunately, this is magic thinking. It may happen that way on television, but not in real life. Transformation in real life takes place both gradually and imperceptibly or violently and rapidly, but it rarely takes place at the speed or in the way we had planned.

In cultures where transformation from one state to another is provoked by initiatory rites, the process is invariably and deliberately painful. Skin is lacerated, bodies are mutilated, the mind is stricken, as if to guarantee that there will be no going back to the way it was before. In our culture, where we have few official initiatory rites, our psyches seem to have found other ways to "lacerate" us into initiation and, perhaps, transformation.

An impossible and passionate love may be one of these ways. In that case, it is more than a romantic fantasy, and it may also be more than just a passing madness, a self-destructive impulse, or a stubborn addiction. Whatever our ignorance or apprehension about its actual reality, it does continue to fascinate us as a cultural ideal and archetype. There must, therefore, be more to understand about it than its dark destruction, or even its sweet beauty. Indeed, as we shall see, in the "impossibility" of certain passions may lie the possibility of initiation into unknown depths of ourselves, of life, and even death.

This sense of "unknown depths" is what pulls us into the enchantment of a great and impossible love story, whether it be told in an old legend or shown in a modern movie. Our minds follow the story, the plot, the development and adventures of the characters, but our psyches respond to the archetypes. They respond to what is eternal and meaningful and universal behind the particular names and places, and in the responding they remind us that we do not just participate in the practical, linear here-and-now, but in the timeless space of myth and feeling and destiny.

If this were not true, we would simply leave the theater or put down the book and forget about it, like a meal enjoyed or a newspaper read. We would not be interested in love tales from another century about people we will never meet. But we are interested, and we don't forget these stories, any more than we forget the ones we live ourselves. How else to make sense of what we live? If impossible love is an initiation, it is not just a private one. It is a collective event, as well, that puts us in touch with aspects of human experience much vaster than our own lives.

What follows is about impossible love from both points of view, the personal one and the collective one. How is it possible to survive and make some sense out of a love affair that erupts between two people, but cannot be lived out? How can we understand the disruptive message of impossible love in the cultural psyche of the world at large? There are no absolute or "right" answers in the pages that follow but rather patterns of experience and conclusions to be drawn from them. Most of all, however, starting with an old and true tale of impossible love upon which many of our modern fantasies are based, there is company, lovers past and present to meet and learn from, as we ask the question *"What for?"*

PART I
Abelard and Heloïse:
Lovers Who Did It Wrong
and Lived to Tell Their Tale

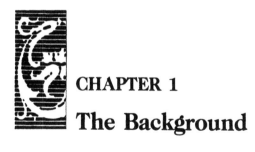

CHAPTER 1

The Background

Their Psychological Relevance for Lovers Today

Our exploration begins with the story of two of the most famous lovers of all, Abelard and Heloïse. She has been called the Woman Who Invented Love. As a couple, Abelard and Heloïse have become legends in our culture and their names synonymous with impossible love. People still put flowers on their joint tomb in the cemetery of Père Lachaise in Paris. Yet, what do we know about these two people, the ones behind the legends, songs, and the frequent sentimentalizing, and why does their story concern us beyond its purely historical value?

As we shall see, Abelard and Heloïse as individuals were even more interesting than the legends that grew up around them and their love affair. Both of them were brilliant and difficult human beings, and their response to the passion that overwhelmed them was totally in character with the person they each had always been. It is for this reason that I have chosen to use their story as a first "case history." Unlike Tristan and Iseult or other famous lovers in our cultural pantheon and imagination, Abelard and Heloïse really existed, had a full life before their meeting and a long life afterwards. They were not just the protagonists of a beautiful tale of impossible love for future generations. What's more, they both left many written documents that tell us exactly how they came to terms, or didn't, with the love affair that changed their lives.[1]

In all these particularities, then, Abelard and Heloïse are much closer to us than the romantic heroes and heroines of pure legend. Yet their story is also "mythic" in the sense that it contains all the universal and archetypal elements of the configuration of impossible love anywhere and any time—the passion, the betrayal, the destruction, the longing, the separation, the bitterness, the transformation, and the unswerving loyalty of both individuals to one truth. The historical distance between them and us gives perspective to our exploration, but the similarities between these two citizens of the twelfth century and our own psyches caught in impossible love turn out to be more numerous than the differences—proof that we participate in unchanging archetypal energies when the "gods" decide it's time for us to be initiated into their worlds.

Like Heloïse and Abelard, most people today have a life before and a life after a great passion or an experience of impossible love. Like Abelard and Heloïse, these people bring their own psychology to the experience as well as their own needs and desires. As we shall see, however, starting with the example of Abelard and Heloïse, these needs and desires are not what they seem to be on the surface. Much to the dismay of the conscious ego-in-love, there turns out to be a very large gap between the original perceived need to be loved, admired, or enfolded, and a strange, deeper psychic need that leads to just the opposite— conflict, longing, misunderstanding, and separation. Abelard and Heloïse, especially Heloïse perhaps, would probably be surprised to hear their story told as an example of psychological necessity, but no more than most of us as we rail against the fates and seek in vain a possible solution to our impossible love problem.

Abelard and Heloïse: Love as a New Value

The mutual passion between Abelard and Heloïse lasted just a few years, and yet it transformed their lives totally, setting each on a path of destruction, struggle, creativity, and exile that neither would have taken without their impossible love. Not only did their passion transform their individual lives, it also contributed to a transformation in our very way of conceiving of love in Western culture. In medieval Europe, they were the first couple to become famous for loving, the first people who left written documents for posterity based on their relationship. Certainly today we all produce documents on relationship in our minds or in our journals or on our computers, but then, in the twelfth century, no one did. Love between women and men was at best a by-product, not a goal or even an expectation in an age when marriages were arranged or determined almost solely by social and economic criteria. By the time the century was over, however, love was to have taken its place as a central value in the European mentality. As Joseph Campbell points out, it was to become a symbol for the Western path of quest and consciousness. In *Creative Mythology*, he writes that this new form of romantic love between men and women was

> love neither as celebration of intercourse or sublimation towards Godhead and neighbor, but as a refining force that *opens the heart* [emphasis mine] to the sad, bittersweet melody of being—through sorrow and joy.[2]

In Christian Europe until that time, love had been dichotomized into good and bad kinds, in opposition to each other. The "bad" kind, of course, was the sexual kind known then as "eros" or lust. It reeked of sin and the devil, and if not controlled it could lead down the "left-hand path, the pagan path of instinct, nature, lust and indiscriminate mating of phallus and womb."[3]

The "good" kind was known as "agape" and consisted of the "sublimation towards Godhead and neighbor" that Campbell describes above. It led away from sin and the left-handed downward path by pointing upwards along the right-handed path toward pure spiritual "caritas." In this dichotomy, sinners fornicated and saints sublimated while human beings did their best to survive and find peace of mind between bodily and spiritual needs.

Emotional needs in this schema were simply not central. The idea of seeking and having a right to emotional fulfillment through relationship is a modern one, and it finds its origins in the new, *third kind of love*—"Amor"—that began to emerge in the twelfth century. From the north of Europe came the legend of Tristan and Iseult, the tragic star-crossed lovers. From the south the troubadours began to sing of the Knight and His Lady in the Courts of Love in Southern France, and in the middle, Abelard and Heloïse met and lived out their "amor." All these lovers were neither on the right-handed path nor the left, but on the path straight ahead of "eyes and heart," a new path of loving not just dictated by instinct or decreed by authority.

What about Abelard and Heloïse made it possible and perhaps inevitable that they would become the "founders" of romantic love, and their passion a prototype of impossible love? To answer this, it is worthwhile looking more closely at their story, for in a way we are all still in the twelfth century in our attempts to come to terms with the mystery of love. In this end of the twentieth century, seven hundred years after the emergence of romantic love, are we not still struggling to differentiate among eros, agape, and amor in our own lives? In this age of sexual liberation on the one hand and obsessions with "caring" relationships on the other, are we not still more often tossed between forms of eros and agape than set on the more individual path of amor? Could it be that sometimes only the burning passion of impossible love teaches us finally to love personally, individually, and deeply? That we need its fire and destruction to burn away the clichés we've hidden behind in the name of fitting in and loving the "right" way, but not necessarily "our" way?

Yet, individuation—or becoming who we most deeply are—is never a right way or a collective enterprise, and neither loving like everyone else nor being sexually liberated like everyone else will lead us to a sense of our own truth. Impossible love may just do this, because it is by definition wrong and puts us outside the norms of our psychic and social milieu. We may resent this and regret it, or we may go with it and grow. Unlike Abelard and Heloïse we will probably not become famous for living an impossible love, but, in today's video-clip world, anyone who wants to can become famous, or infamous, at least for a day. It's not necessarily a sign of individuation. However, like Abelard and Heloïse, through an impossible love we may touch on something "great" within, including a deeper connection to our own truth. Like them, we may come face to face with the reality that we are not who we thought we were, and that we cannot go on living our lives in exactly the same way we always have.

With their permission then, granted by their own published correspondence, let us see what it was like for them and why, in spite of several hundred years' distance, we would probably have no trouble sharing experiences with them, be it in a religious community of twelfth-century France or in a self-help group of urban twentieth-century North America.

CHAPTER 2
Their Story

Their Meeting and Passion

Even before they met, both Abelard and Heloïse were exceptional for their time, and each had come a long way from the confines of the worlds into which they had been born.

Abelard (b.1079) was the oldest son of a Breton knight.[1] Brittany was not yet part of France, and it would have been most unusual for an oldest son to leave his Celtic roots in order to study elsewhere, especially in Paris, the seat of Latin learning and Church power. Abelard did just that, however. His father, though a man of arms, was a lover of culture as well and exposed his children early to the world of learning. Abelard turned out to be so gifted and so interested in his studies that he decided to give up his inheritance and become a scholar. In his own words, "I left the Court of Mars to grow in the arms of Minerva."[2] By leaving the God of War in order to serve the Goddess of Wisdom, he broke with the past and set out on a course that would inevitably lead him to the Great Schools of Paris, and from there into the arms of Heloïse and a destiny quite different from that which either his own father or he himself could have foreseen.

As for Heloïse, born in 1101 when Abelard had already become a famous Peripatetic, or wandering scholar, she too was unusual from the beginning.[3] First of all, she was an orphan, who was adopted and brought up by her Uncle Fulbert, the Canon of Notre Dame in Paris. For reasons history doesn't explain to us, Fulbert decided to educate his niece in a way no women and few men were educated in the twelfth century. Aided by her natural gifts and his encouragement, by the time she was a teenager she was already a phenomenon for her time, an erudite, learned woman. Fulbert took great pride in his accomplished niece and enjoyed basking in the fame her brilliance brought him. We can imagine that a large part of his pride was for his own reflected glory, what we would call today narcissistic projection, and not because he foresaw or planned any particular unfolding of her own individuality. In fact, in spite of the education he gave her, if Heloïse had not met Abelard, she probably would have led the typical life of a woman of her class and time. Since there were no career opportunities for women in the twelfth century, no matter how brilliant she was, her fame would probably have subsided once she was married off to a man chosen by Fulbert. With luck, her husband would have at least appreciated his wife's unusual abilities, but more probably her gifts would have simply served to flatter her uncle's name before being buried by the roles of subservient wife and dutiful reproducer of her husband's line.

Heloïse did meet Abelard, however, and every-thing changed for them both. When they met in 1118, she was a young woman of eighteen, he was a man of thirty-nine. Two years later, they became student and teacher, and lovers soon after. Ironically, but not accidentally, they met through Uncle Fulbert.

Abelard was by now a "star" in the Parisian world of learning and scholarship. With his unusual intelli-gence and equally powerful ambition, he had arrived, so to speak, securing a prestigious chair at the School of Paris by unseating his mentor, Guillaume, the Arch-bishop of Paris. He was adored by his students, adulated by the Parisian public—always avid, even then, for clever speakers—and he was cordially detested by many colleagues whom he had either betrayed or humiliated in his ascent to power and glory. His ideas were both original and controversial, and he loved being the center of intellectual debate and dispute. Not for him any false modesty or anxi-ety about success. He called himself the best and believed it. Describing his early teaching years he writes, "From the very first courses I gave, my reputa-tion as a dialectician took on such proportions that not only was the fame of my former colleagues eclipsed but that of my master as well. This success increased my confidence even more."[4] Whatever detractors he had, he dismissed by pointing out that "only the peaks of the mounts attract the lightning."[5]

In spite of professing allegiance to Minerva, in fact Abelard remained close to Mars all his life. He may have given up knighthood and the life of the sword, but he was still a warrior—a warrior of ideas and words with a self-given mission to conquer people's minds and change their ways of thinking about the world itself.

Like a warrior too, Abelard had not, when he met Heloïse, spent much time in such peace-time activities as socializing and cultivating the art of living. All his energy had gone into honing his mind into a perfect arm in order to cut through what he considered outdated and useless ideas advocated by the Church Establishment. The rest of his energy went into intrigues and power plays in order to be a member of this very Establishment, and to have a forum from which to continue his intellectual campaign against the dogmatic thinking he so decried.

By the time he met Heloïse, however, he was, in his own words, already slackening. In "Letter to a Friend" he writes, "seeing myself as the only real philosopher on earth and fearing nothing for the future, I began to let go to my passions, I who had always lived most temperately."[6] The glory had gone to his head; he had begun to rest on his laurels. Instead of maintaining the Spartan discipline that had served him so well in his trajectory, he began to give in to what he calls the twin temptations "of pride and lust."[7]

As is the case with many heroes, Abelard fell more a victim to his own success, vanity, and feeling of invincibility than to any outer forces. As is also the case for many a hero, however, the "fall" allowed for new and unexpected parts of his personality to come forth. We would say today that both his shadow and his anima were finally emerging. First, the shadow of the disciplined intellectual he had always been began to appear as the sensual, instinctual, irrational Dionysian part of his personality that had been relegated to the unconscious, ready to emerge when the vigilance of the warrior ego began to relax. Then the anima, or feminine part of his psyche, claimed her due when, enamored of Heloïse, Abelard began feeling and imagining instead of always fighting, competing, and performing. Weakened by his own vanity, he fell first into a sensual Don Juan and then into a passionate lover. The philosopher of Reason turned into a poet of Amor.

Consciously, this was not at all his intent, especially the latter. Consciously, he simply wanted contact with a woman after all these years of abstinence and heroic effort. With middle age, he began to be aware of his lack of any social life outside the world of intellectual jousting, and his choice fell naturally on Heloïse to be the object of this new undertaking. Word of her brilliance had reached him, and she seemed a likely choice for a star such as he. In fact, like a warrior, Abelard set out to conquer her for his own glory and devised a campaign to gain entrance to her house and eventually her bed.

Here, Fulbert, due to his vanity, came to the aid of Abelard, much to his undying regret. For Fulbert, like most educated Parisians of the time, was a great admirer of the famous theologian and philosopher. How could he resist when Abelard, in the role of a scholar too distracted to manage his own household, prevailed upon Fulbert to rent him a room and to allow him to give Heloïse lessons as a way to contribute to the rent? Abelard knew perfectly well that Fulbert had two loves—his money and his niece.[8] By offering to add to the first and to educate the second, he made himself quite irresistible to Fulbert's greed and vanity. But Abelard's trick turned against him. He fooled Fulbert all right and gained entrance to both the schoolroom and then the heart and bed of Heloïse. But the role of seducer did not last long. In spite of his cynical intentions, Abelard fell into his own trap. He fell madly, passionately in love. As for Heloïse, if she had been an innocent schoolgirl when they first met, with a typical schoolgirl crush on the great scholar, by the time the first few lessons were over she was more than his match in passion. In this domain, they were both just beginners, initiating each other into the world of the senses and the heart.

Their rapture carried them both away, but he, even more than she, totally lost his head. Perhaps because he had more head to lose, i.e., years of living and working and producing from the intellect. She, on the other hand, had had all to gain, at least in her own mind. For Heloïse, a feeling of her own great destiny had walked in the door when Abelard appeared in her chaste schoolroom quarters, and she was not a woman to let a great destiny escape. While he neglected his classes, forgot his professorial duties, lost his interest in great debates, and started for the first time in his life to write poetry and love songs, she gave herself totally to their passion, having no duties to neglect or professional reputation to keep. There was, of course, the question of her reputation as a young woman of good family, but this, extraordinarily enough for a woman of her background and social milieu, did not concern Heloïse at all. *They both infringed taboos by consenting to their love, but their "crime" had different ramifications for each at the time and a different meaning for them both afterwards.*

Such was clear from the minute Heloïse became pregnant and their passion was discovered. Far from being ashamed and afraid as most young women of her station would have been, Heloïse was ecstatic and openly proclaimed herself to be "transported with joy" at her pregnancy.[9] Just as Abelard had reveled in the dangerous pleasures of intellectual opposition to the Church in his younger days, so did Heloïse seem to revel in the dangers and challenges of her new situation.

Abelard, older, with more to lose and less investment in love as an absolute in his life, was less enthusiastic. After all, the truths nearest to his heart had always been and would remain intellectual ones, not ones of the heart and feeling. While the passion he shared with Heloïse clearly exalted her, it threatened more and more to ruin him. He had already lost his invincible arrogance and perfect professional armor through the softening effect of love. Now, with the public discovery of their love, he could lose his reputation and credibility as well. To do him credit, he did the best he could. He took Heloïse away to Brittany to have their child and cared for and protected her during this time.[10] He also proposed to marry her to repair her honor and to make amends to Fulbert, in spite of the almost certain consequences of such an arrangement for him. Marriage, he knew, would mean an end to his career, for although celibacy was not yet universally required of the clergy—only of monks—

it was already a status symbol in the Church hierarchy, at least in appearance. To be sure, many high-placed Church teachers and authorities had concubines and mistresses. This was known and tacitly allowed. But none were married. In such a patriarchal world, prestige and honors were not accorded to men who shared their lives, their names, and especially their hearts with women.

Abelard knew this but still wanted to marry Heloïse. Heloïse knew it and refused to marry him. She cried out against becoming a "mere wife," saying she would rather be his lover or mistress than become a millstone around his neck, saddling him with children and family responsibilities.[11] She preferred by far that her lover continue fulfilling his glorious destiny of great teacher and thinker, so that she could serve him and his destiny from her heart, not because of a legal tie.

Today we would raise our eyebrows at such a romantic notion. We know too many examples of women who have sacrificed their own security and creativity, leaving all to abet the destiny of a loved man, to believe that such a sacrifice can lead much further than lack of fulfillment and mutual bitterness. Today we would urge the woman to withdraw her animus projections and get on with her own life rather than put all her ambitions on to the object of her love. We might even suggest that a desire such as she expressed was a sign of avoidance behavior and fear of success.

Heloïse, however, had no therapist to mirror back her words, much less her desire. But even if she had, the words would have been foreign to her. She was getting on with her own life and she knew it. The choice for her was clear—love or marriage—and it was a choice at least as heart-rending for her as the choice can be for anyone today who must choose between a lover's needs and her own. Marriage then was the collective way, the only way for women except the convent. There were no women who by choice remained unmarried and yet in a love affair. For Heloïse, therefore, to fight her lover in order not to get married was revolutionary.

Unfortunately, it was too revolutionary for the men in her life, her uncle and her lover. Pressure from both finally got the best of her, but when she finally did accede to the marriage it was with great misgiving and announcement of catastrophe: "It is the only thing we have left to do in order to lose each other and ready ourselves for a grief as great as our love."[12]

She was right. For no sooner had the marriage taken place in order for Abelard to prove to the world his sense of honor, then Fulbert began to go back on his promise of forgiveness of both niece and lover. He harassed and persecuted Heloïse so much that Abelard had to take and hide her in a convent outside of Paris. And no sooner had he done that than he himself was attacked by Fulbert's men. Back in Paris, alone in his bed, with Heloïse out of danger and his own life in a shambles, Abelard was held down and castrated by the avenging menfolk of Heloïse's family. End of passion. Beginning of a new destiny for each of the lovers.

Abelard fled Paris, took refuge in a monastery, and took vows to become a monk. He enjoined Heloïse to do the same, and out of love for him, not vocation, she did. They remained married, but rarely saw each other over the following twenty-three years of Abelard's life. He died in 1142, and she was to outlive him by twenty-one years. Over these years their lives intersected, but they were never again to meet as lovers. Most of what we know about their lives comes from the letters that she wrote to him, and the letters he wrote to a friend in the form of a booklet called "Letter to a Friend or Story of My Calamities." The title is significant, and so is the fact that he wrote these very personal and passionate missives about his life, not to his wife and former lover, but to a male friend.

This is just one example of how far they were to go from each other in their perception of the value and importance of their mutual passion. The years after their separation were extremely difficult for both, and they both were forced to find different ways to cope with their difficulties. For Heloïse the love of Abelard would remain the central and guiding passion in her life in spite of the veil she had accepted. For Abelard their love would become the catastrophe that changed his life for the worse and set him on a very different road from the one he had aspired to.

Heloïse Afterwards

Heloïse's life was outwardly calmer than Abelard's in these years. Having taken the veil at his insistence, she eventually became abbess of the Order of the Paraclet, a religious community for women that

Abelard founded in order to create a situation of security and dignity for her. It was also a way for him to put her once and for all into a new relationship with him. As abbess, she became a "sister-in-God" as far as he was concerned, and he named himself her spiritual director, thus ensuring the transformation from carnal passion and "amor" to spiritual "agape." As we shall see, Heloïse alternated between submitting to the repression of her erotic and emotional femininity and revolting against it. We know little of her actual daily life and accomplishments except that she became famous as an abbess for her intelligence, devotion, compassion, and learning. We know also from the letters she exchanged with Abelard in her role as obedient sister-in-God that she was concerned about finding new ways for women to live in convents and serve their faith.

She pointed out to him in these letters that the rules she and her charges were supposed to follow had been originally conceived for men and that not all of them, particularly those concerning hygiene and physical work, were suitable or appropriate for women.[13] In her way, she was very ahead of her time, almost a feminist in her insistence on the dignity and rights of the women in her charge. She was also ahead of her time in her concern for education for women and in her explorations of the particular contributions they could make to their order, as well as to the world around them.

We know this of Heloïse, and we can admire her independence of mind and the intelligence she brought to these issues in her discussion of them with Abelard as her spiritual director. Of her emotional and personal life in the convent, however, we know next to nothing. We do not know if she had friends, conflicts, disappointments, or satisfactions in her daily life. Since her letters to Abelard are the only written documents we have from her, we only have evidence of the overriding emotion in her life—her love for him—adamant and passionate or subdued and discreet, but constant. If she had other emotional upheavals or concerns, she censured them or put them aside to concentrate on this one central ideal. Because of this, our picture of Heloïse is much more one-sided than the view we have of Abelard. We have few glimpses of her "shadow," the darker side of her personality—the possible moments of pettiness, disloyalty, abuse of power in her role of abbess, or other human failings. For the most part, from her letters we just have her "light"—her passion, commitment, and courage in the face of the terribly painful relationship with Abelard.

Abelard Afterwards

If we look to Abelard's life and story after their passion, a different and more complex picture emerges. On the one hand, we have more objective historical information about his life in exile because he remained active in Church circles where history was being written. On the other hand, we have the personal documents Abelard wrote to his male friend. From both of these sources we learn that his life, unlike that of Heloïse, turned into a series of outer catastrophes as well as inner torture.

Castrated and humiliated, he took refuge from Paris in various monasteries throughout France and Brittany. He did not, however, take refuge in silence. Alone and embittered, he nonetheless kept writing, thinking, and fulminating against official Church thought. In fact, he did so more than ever before. From being a great warrior of ideas and a seducer of minds, he turned into a crusader and reformer. He apparently set out not only to change the thinking of Church theologians, but to clean up the behavior of all the monks in the different monasteries he visited and had charge of over the years. As a result, he made enemies not only among the powerful in Paris but among the very people who took him in in his disgrace. However, no number of enemies could discourage Abelard. Instead, his painful situation fostered in him a fanaticism that fed on adversity and would not leave him until his death. To comfort himself in his solitude, he often compared himself to St. Augustine, the great sinner who had seen the light and given all to God. In fact, his troubles just added to his feelings of misunderstood greatness, and he thanked God for having removed the temptations of lust and pride so he could devote himself solely to God's service.[14]

More specifically, this service consisted of bringing the light into the benighted souls of those who resisted his reforms or refused his ideas. We see him in all his fanaticism and small-mindedness as he accuses those around him of betrayal and obtuseness.

He complains, laments, and feels sorry for himself. Unlike Heloïse, he does not come across as a greater human being for having loved. Yet, intellectually, he continued to grow, and his ideas became the obsession which kept him alive, just as Heloïse's passion for him sustained her.

Although remembered more today for his unhappy love affair than for his scholarship, Abelard did in fact initiate a deep change in the thought of his times and contributed to opening up the medieval mind to the future. He was the first of his century to publicly and insistently praise the ancients—especially Aristotle—for their scientific approach to nature, and this at a time when Greek philosophy was banned from the Church as so much "pagan" heresy. He opposed reason to revelation and dialectics to dogma at a time when the Church was entirely invested and immersed in unquestioning theological traditionalism.[15] He would have been more at home in the France of the Age of Enlightenment than the France of the Middle Ages, for he was virtually alone in taking a stand of such intellectual daring. Paradoxically, in the aftermath of his affair with Heloïse, he, like her, went on to express ideas far ahead of his own time.

The Couple Afterwards

Tragically, the revolutionary ideas and ideals that kept each of the lovers alive also separated them more and more from each other.

The blaze of passion that had united them so absolutely for a moment also transformed their lives absolutely, but it transformed them separately. The couple they had been did not continue to evolve as One. Their marriage did not provide a unifying third entity. On the contrary, it split them apart and made them evolve alone, sometimes willingly, sometimes reluctantly, but always separately.

While his wife defended Love and blamed him for his negligence of her, Abelard defended Reason and blamed the religious authorities for their neglect of him and for all his worldly woes. To paraphrase James Hillman, the two lovers "worshipped at different altars."[16] They had, unknowingly, very different visions about what the truth was and which truth mattered most. Yet, both their truths would resonate down through the ages—she the Spokeswoman for Love, he the Spokesman for Logic and Reason, each separate and exceptional at the end as they had been in the beginning.

Indeed, it was as if their unusual destinies required the destructive effect of their passion to be shaped and articulated into two original and separate visions. More than anything, this tragedy of *two separate truths that lie immovable behind the appearance of one love* emerges as the source of the most creative and the most destructive elements in the experience of an impossible love. It also lends a different light to the usual way of assessing the value of certain relationships between lovers, as we shall see in looking at the particular characteristics of the love relationship between Abelard and Heloïse.

CHAPTER 3

A Look at Their Relationship

Abelard in Flight

If we look at the love affair between Abelard and
Heloïse purely from the point of view of today's Relationship values, then at first it would seem that
Abelard was simply a cad and Heloïse a victim—no
matter what the truths they each held to.

It is very easy to read her letters to him as those
of a woman seduced and abandoned. It's easy to read
his missives to her as the products of a wounded nar-
cissist who betrayed his love in order to regain his self-
esteem, or to restore his persona, as we might say. As
a lover, he did in fact behave abjectly, turning her en-
treaties to him as a man into requests for spiritual
direction, addressing her always as his "sister-in-God,"
never as his wife or lover. He denies her passion,
refuses to hear her pain, and adds insult to injury by
expressing amazement at the fact that she could claim
to be so needy.

When he finally answers her letters, it is by opening with these words:

If I have not written one letter of consolation or exhortation to you since we both took leave of the world for God, you must not think it due to any neglect on my part but rather to the absolute confidence I have in your wisdom. I never believed that any help would be necessary to one like you whom God has blessed with all the gifts of grace.[1]

The modern-day version might be "What do you mean you feel hurt, or pained, or abandoned; you are so strong, so together, you can't have those feelings." Of course, the real message is that "I can't or won't hear about your pain. It makes me feel too guilty."

It was as if he could not and would not re-enter the relationship with her as man, lover, and equal. He either condescended to her, berating her weakness, or used her for his own weakness. This was especially evident when, in the thrall of one of the more dramatic moments of persecution by different Church authorities, Abelard sought refuge with Heloïse and the sisters of the Order he had founded for her. There, in Paraclet, he was taken in and cared for. At the same time, students came from all over France to show their devotion and loyalty while the great man recovered and basked in the loving care of the women. He had turned them all, including his wife, into disciples, Mary Magdalenes and Virgin Marys, devoted sister and loving mother. This, of course, is exactly what Heloïse complained about. She was pained by being forced into a role she did not want with him and out of one she did, and her hurt was justified.

The attitude of Abelard was one not original to him, however. It is the attitude of many a disenchanted lover, man or woman, who disowns love and proposes another, less engaging level of rapport. While Abelard proposed and imposed that he and Heloïse be sister and brother in God, today one would say, "Let's be friends." Feeling perfectly magnanimous, such a person manages to both wound and insult far more than if he or she had simply said, "I don't love you anymore." But Abelard, like many people, could not openly own such "shadow" feelings. He needed to see himself as good and pure, not as unloving and treacherous. He also needed to keep Heloïse in the wings for when he was feeling especially unloved by the rest of the world, and so, under guise of not causing pain and being concerned with her spiritual welfare, he managed to break her heart as well as to deny his own connection to amor.

Heloïse on Fire

And what about Heloïse: was she truly only the wronged woman, led astray, ruined, and victimized by her charismatic lover? Heroine of love and suffering in spite of herself? As we follow her through the years of separation and then communication, we begin to see that in fact her "truth of love" could be just as obsessive and denying of the Other as Abelard's own rejection of love for Reason and what he called their "spiritual destiny."[2]

Heloïse began to write to Abelard only after his

"Story of My Calamities" appeared in public and came to her attention. Till then she had been silent, enduring her lot, building up the order Abelard had entrusted to her care, seeing him occasionally as a fellow member of the religious community, not expressing her love openly or addressing her lover publicly. But when the manuscript of the "Calamities" became known to her, Heloïse could contain herself no longer. The dam holding back the feelings and suffering she had so heroically quelled broke, and she took up pen to respond to his publicized lamentations.

Her opening remarks reflect his difficulties and empathize with them. Like any lover, she wants first of all to establish a special complicity. Thus, she implores him to write directly to her about his problems so she can sympathize and offer support. After these overtures, however, she begins to make a claim for her own feelings. She subtly reminds him of his debt to her as an unswervingly loyal friend through all these years, and then less subtly opens up into their passion. Her own pain breaks through at this point. She reminds him that she only took the veil to please him, not out of any desire of her own or any true vocation. She even dares to reproach him for using her, seducing her, and then leaving her; and she extols the greatness of her own love for which she has given up all worldly pleasures—the brilliant Parisian life she could have led—all for love of him alone. Interspersed with descriptions of her pain is flattery: she lists his charms and the uniqueness of his great intellectual talent as worthy objects for such a love as hers.[3] In other words, she feeds his narcissism while trying to have her own wound acknowledged, but this is exactly what Abelard will not do.

Unlike Abelard, Heloïse could not and did not want to take refuge in spiritual sublimation. She was intensely, passionately female and human in her love and, once touched by its arrow, wanted to go on touching and being touched by love in all of her being and body. She would certainly understand these modern twentieth-century words about touching:

> To touch, to reach beneath the armour, beneath the
> earth,
> down among the roots of being,
> To touch the buried moods, poems, dreams,
> The seeds of soaring possibilities.[4]

They are words about another intimate relationship—psychoanalysis—but they could also express the hope of every love affair, to reach through the armor and find "amor." To be touched and "to touch the untouchable and the untouched."[5]

For a while, this was the kind of love that Abelard and Heloïse lived together. Both were touched by their passion, and through it both felt new possibilities arising from within. The philosopher became a poet, the schoolgirl became a heroine. In his "Calamities," Abelard acknowledges how deeply the armor was pierced and unfamiliar feelings stirred when he admits that, faced with the impossibility of their love, "With a broken heart I wept over the fate of it and what sobs of pain did she weep at my dishonor. Each wept for the catastrophe of the other."[6] At that moment he was touched. Later he would no longer let himself be touched; he would go on to pursue his other Truth, much to the everlasting chagrin of Heloïse, who was forced to go on loving by herself. She really was the Woman Who Invented Love, as the French call her, but she "invented" it alone in the years in the convent.

Reading Heloïse's letters, we see that the proud, brilliant young woman who was ready to face social ostracism rather than capitulate to social pressure to marry her lover is still in later life just as proud and brilliant. She matches Abelard's theological erudition point for point, refuses to be treated as a mere "sister-in-God," and insists, despite his defensive distancing, on making her love heard. Up until the end, she will claim that her love for Abelard makes her more the spouse of the man than the bride of Christ—a shocking statement for the abbess of a Catholic convent.[7] And never does she write a word of regret or remorse about their love.

While Abelard exhorts Heloïse to embrace "*la grande destinée*" that their marriage and flight from the world opened up to them—

> See how greatly God has cared for us as if He had reserved us for a great destiny, as if it would have grieved or upset Him to know that the treasures of knowledge he confided to us both were not used in honor of His name and as if He had feared the wantonness of his servant.[8]

—she insists that her own *grande destinée* is to serve

him: "You are the one and only master of my heart as well as of my body."[9] Serving him becomes more and more, however, a question of serving an idea of him. With no personal acknowledgment of her feelings, Heloïse has no choice but to address herself increasingly to an ideal Abelard, one she has set up in her mind as the perfect object of her love. In Jungian terms, we would say Abelard has become a pure animus, an inner figure of masculine energy in Heloïse's own psyche. The empirical Abelard may be petty and disloyal and ungrateful in their relationship, and it may be hopeless for her to attempt to touch him with her feelings as a woman, but Heloïse can and does keep her pride and sanity by returning to the idealized image of him as the intellectual hero of her youth. She stubbornly holds on to her love—in spite of her lover.

On the outside, however, Heloïse seems to give in to his refusal to acknowledge the carnal, human love between them. Little by little, she adapts the tone of her letters to that of a colleague and sister in religion. The last letters between them, "The Letters of Direction," concern only a discussion of points of theology and the different reforms and changes that Heloïse wants to bring to the women's orders. In these exchanges, they are equals. Abelard respects her learning and judgments as she argues and elaborates points of procedure regarding the feminine religious communities. It would seem that she has accepted his terms in order to maintain the relationship. Yet, through certain reactions and statements, we can see how absolutely unchanged she is in her inner feelings.

When, near the end of his life, Abelard recants

some of his own ideas in order to be pardoned by the Church, Heloïse responds with furor and alacrity. She cannot believe her hero has actually done such a thing, as if he has no right to be human, to be weak and tired.[10] She, after all, has sacrificed her life and energy to a task she would not have chosen for herself, but accepted because of him. She has accepted his defection from their passion. She cannot, besides, accept his defection from the role he defended, hid behind, and that she, "*faute de mieux*," came to idealize—the role of Thinker, Philosopher, Revolutionary of the Mind.

In her reaction, we see how far the two have come from each other. We see that in fact neither was able to really see and acknowledge the other person's human reality. Abelard fled Heloïse and turned her into a reluctant saint. Heloïse made a cult of Abelard and transformed him into an Invincible Hero of the Mind. Neither could hear or acknowledge the fear and pain of the other when it was outside their own concerns. They engaged more and more in what the French call a "*dialogue de sourdes*," a dialogue of the deaf. Both idealized the image of the other in order to nourish another, deeper ideal. *The impossible was not only an outer reality separating two star-crossed lovers, but it became an inner reality making them deaf to each other's world and making a "real" relationship impossible to re-establish.*

Happy Endings Aren't Everything

As we observe these developments, we can still conclude that it was all Abelard's fault since he "made" her leave him to go into another world and another fate. Yet, to blame him for failure in the relationship would be to overlook the value of what each actually accomplished and became. It would be to ignore how powerful a person Heloïse became in her own right and to wish she had never written a letter. Finally, and most important, it would be to put the notion of Happy Ending on a pedestal, taking away the dignity and depth of their experience.

This, of course, is the problem in our modern way of seeing all romantic encounters as headed for only one of two possible endings: either to finish abusively, with one partner exploiting and seducing the other, or to end happily, with the partners together forever in mutual and consistent caring and support. Emotional mugging or affective social security. Yet, as actual lovers know, there are far more elements to coupleness than abuse of power or absolute security and mutuality.

Some relationships are healing or comforting, others are stimulating and maddening, still others are creative and destructive at the same time. All of these and more may have their purpose and meaning in our lives at a given time, and may be lived with the same person or with many. More than any other, however, impossible love relationships put us on a level of transcendent feelings and values, both heavenly and diabolic. If they "work," that is, if the impossibility becomes a spur to transformation and not just bitterness, then we may end up revising our whole belief system in order to contain the intensity of the relationship that has no happy ending in the outer world.

Returning to Abelard and Heloïse, we would propose that the separate truths that each carried were not just isolated ideals that arose out of a failed relationship. They evolved, in fact, out of very deep previous belief systems that had been profoundly changed and colored by their passion together.

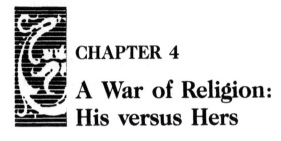

CHAPTER 4

A War of Religion: His versus Hers

From Collective Belief to Personal Heresy

Our lovers could not let in each other's world, because to do so would have been to threaten an entire belief system upon which each of their lives had been constructed. As Hillman points out, "When people fall in love not only eyes and lips and hearts meet but theologies. We come to the encounter not only with love but also with an *idea of love.*"[1] In other words, our ideas have just as much to do with the outcome of our love lives as our feelings, especially when these ideas turn around "subjects of ultimate concern." This, according to the *Webster's Third International Dictionary*, is what makes up a theology—"the sum of beliefs of a group or individual regarding religious faith or matters of *ultimate concern.*"[2]

In these matters of vital concern to ourselves, we all have our theologies, whether we realize it or not. Whatever the "gods" or highest values that guide us, there will be our beliefs as well. Power, money, love, relationship, work—these are but a few of the guiding forces behind which stand the transpersonal values that we adhere to and build on in creating our inner theologies. According to our philosophy, we might worship at the temple of Mammon, God, Aphrodite, or the Great Mother without ever realizing which altar we are at most of the time. It is only when these altars are threatened that we turn into zealots or missionaries, preaching our truths as if they were the only truths.

To look at the story of Abelard and Heloïse from this point of view is to better understand the drama and impossibility of their love. Before the passion that smote them and shattered their lives, they had each belonged to and adhered to institutions that imposed the collective values of their time—the Church and society. Although they were each unusual in their milieu—a young woman educated far beyond the norm and a man who used his intellect to provoke the norms—each was also entirely integrated into his or her own world. In those worlds, everything had its place. Church theology determined social convention. It defined the roles of women and men in the world and decreed what degrees of reward or punishment would accompany those adhering to or departing from its authority. Paradise, purgatory, and hell were the same for all Christians, including Abelard and Heloïse.

By falling in love, however, Abelard and Heloïse fell out of this ordered collective system. They lost their membership in the official order and were forced to evolve in what would become an increasingly individual belief system. They both, in a manner of speaking, became heretics in relation to the conventions and beliefs that dictated their lives before their passion. But even there, even in heresy, they diverged from one another.

Abelard's heresy was official, one regarding the *nature* of the divinity. In exile, he was to go on challenging the very idea of God's exact nature as presented by Church dogma, pointing out that Reason was as important as faith in the work of theological understanding, and he would be condemned as a heretic for such ideas.[3] Heloïse's "heresy," on the other hand, though never called so officially, would be even greater than his, for hers would be to challenge the very *identity* of the divinity. By raising love between man and woman to the level of the sacred and putting her lover before the figure of Christ himself, she was even more radical than Abelard.

Separated from each other, banished from the collective, and in exile from the major sources of power, both lovers went deeper and deeper into their own individual theologies. Both felt they had fallen out of Paradise into endless purgatory, and sometimes Hell. Their purgatories and hells, however, were different, because their idea of paradise had been different from the beginning.

Separate Salvation, Separate Damnation

The paradise of Abelard had been a world of intellectual triumph, stimulation, and glory. He lived his passion with Heloïse not as a new paradise and a new religion, but as a delightful diversion and then a disorienting shock. It took him into the pleasures of feelings and the senses, but ultimately it became the agent of the devil that destroyed his manhood and his reputation and alienated him forever from the paradise of power and fame. Not for nothing did he deny his love and condemn his own passion in later years, lamenting, "I burned for you with all the flames of desire to the point of preferring to God and to myself those miserable and impure acts of lust that I would now blush to call by their name."[4] For him love had been the doorway to hell and exile, and though he never accused Heloïse of being at fault, he certainly sounds in these later years more like Adam complaining after the Fall than the poet d'amor he had so briefly been.

Heloïse, on the other hand, had no such regrets. In *her* theology, their love affair had been paradise. Not only did she experience the rapture of sensual awakening and first love, but all this with Abelard, the object of her greatest admiration, a divinity in the sky of her intellectual aspirations. Her passion with him gave her the opportunity to show her courage, her mettle, her fire in a way few other experiences could have done. It was, as the Church says of the mystic's experience, "self-verifying," justifying her existence beyond and without the usual social conventions that tell us who we are and where we belong. By being chosen as Abelard's lover, Heloïse rose above all womankind, at least in her own eyes, and found a cause equal to her brilliance and the passion of her temperament. Memories of passion with Abelard became her "Paradise Lost"; her passion for the cause of their love became her way of trying to re-create Paradise.

She had been right in predicting that for them to get married would bring about their mutual doom and "a grief as great as our love," but she had not foreseen what type of doom. In her mind, hell would have been the banality of marriage, with its charges of children and household things that would weigh down Abelard and turn her from a goddess of love into a "mere" housewife, a role she did not relish for herself. She could not have foreseen that the end of paradise brought about by their marriage would in fact be the purgatory of loneliness and the hell of separation from each other. Still, Heloïse's fears of marriage had been grounded. While Abelard had hoped that marriage would allow them to stay in paradise, i.e., in an unchanged world like before, Heloïse knew marriage would end it.

Is it any surprise when we see how divergent their very ideas of love and paradise were from the beginning, that, once the lovers separated, these views diverged even more, building into the solid and separate truths they each were to defend the rest of their lives?

Failed Love, Successful Lives

Ironically, one could also say that Abelard, in seeing the "great destiny" in the very separation Heloïse so deplored, was as right as she was in seeing their separation as doom. It is a fact that the heresy they both espoused in their exile, and the powerful beliefs they evolved and defended, carried tremendous energy back into the world. Out of an outer wilderness and inner despair and love for Abelard, Heloïse created an order for women that would be a model of enlightened attitudes toward women, as well as service to the community. Though her letters to Abelard reveal mostly the hurt lover, and then the obedient "sister-in-God," she continued to be known and admired throughout France as a woman of exceptional leadership and learning.

Fate and society threw her out of Abelard's arms, but also out of the predictable, comfortable life she would have otherwise lived as a learned, well-born woman of her time, and into the unexpected roles of writer, lover, and leader. Annoyed as she would be to read this, her real originality started only after the separation. Without it, she could easily have been just a smitten schoolgirl wronged and then righted by her lover like hundreds of others, before and since. The affair would have caused a scandal and been forgotten as she took up the responsibilities of her social standing, either married to Abelard or taken back by her uncle. We would never have heard of Abelard and Heloïse; she would not be known as the Woman Who Invented Love. Of course, she would have been happy to sacrifice such a reputation just to be by her lover's side and serve him, instead of his memory, but the world would probably have been poorer.

As for Abelard, would he have gone so far and been so recklessly adamant in his ideas if he had stayed in Paris happily attended by a devoted mistress and otherwise taken up by the demands of fame and fortune? Since we cannot re-write their lives, it is impossible to say whether either would have gone as far into their individual voices and truths if their love had been possible and their respective paradises not lost. Nevertheless, we can see in their love story, as it actually evolved, several themes of creativity that sometimes emerge from the destructiveness of impossible love.

CHAPTER 5
Creativity and Paradise Lost

Abelard and Creative Illness

For something new to be born, paradise must be lost. This is as true for the child leaving the womb as it is for the work of art leaving the safety of the mind of its creator in order to take form in the world. Birth is painful; the creative force rapes our inner virginity and challenges the untouched, unquestioned beliefs, putting us in touch with chaos and darkness before it leads, if ever, to renewal or regeneration.

Abelard's life is a striking example of a creative person's descent into this darkness and psychic death. Reading the litany of his self-pitying miseries brings to mind what Henri Ellenberger relates about Freud, another revolutionary thinker, and his particular "creative illness." Ellenberger points out in his book *The Discovery of the Unconscious* that, for many innovative thinkers such as Freud, it is almost a psychological necessity to feel misunderstood and isolated. For example, even though Freud was in a stable marriage, well supported financially by his private practice, and admired by many colleagues, he still experienced himself as alone. Even after the publication of his seminal book *Interpretation of Dreams*, there "remained the impression of having passed through a long period of terrible isolation in a hostile world."[1] Ellenberger goes on to define such a creative illness as follows:

> A creative illness precedes a period of intense preoccupation with an idea, and a search for truth. The symptoms may be depression, paranoia, neurosis, psychosomatic manifestations. Throughout, the subject never loses the thread of the dominating preoccupation and is almost entirely absorbed by himself. There is throughout a conviction of having discovered a grandiose truth that must be proclaimed to mankind.[2]

In many cases, I would venture to say that such symptoms do not just precede, but accompany, the entire creative struggle, and thus this description would certainly fit Abelard in all the years of his intellectual production and campaigning after his exile from Paris. In fact, despite his complaints, his productivity and creativity grew during these troubled years. He was fanatically attached to his ideas and to the need to put them into the world—not for money, not for power and glory which he had lost through his passion with Heloïse, but for the ideas themselves. In this sense, we could say that both he and Freud had what Jung would call a truly "religious attitude"—an attitude of devotion and fidelity to something greater than oneself.

This would certainly surprise both men—the nine-
teenth-century scientist who disdained religion as the
opium of the people and the twelfth-century monk
for whom religion was a structural given, not something to be proven by any particular attitude or creativity. Yet Abelard's true religion was his own inner truth,
no matter how much he professed humility in the service of God. His penitential suffering, though real, was
never as absolute as he made it out to be. We know
from Heloïse's letters, in fact, that there were always
a great number of students and admirers who stayed
loyal to Abelard and were only too happy to help him
whenever he would let them. They even constructed
with their own hands the buildings for the order he
founded, Paraclet, of which Heloïse would be the abbess. But Abelard rather conveniently forgot both their
devotion and the continued support of Heloïse as he
turned again and again to the fight with his enemies.
This was what kept him going and drove him to produce treatise after treatise—ever a warrior, ever a
crusader, reveling in his hardships, lamenting his trials,
but unable to exist without them.

He, unlike Freud, was not comfortably well-off in
a bourgeois residence of a sophisticated modern city.
Yet one wonders if it would have made any difference.
If one compares the two men, Freud and Abelard, and
sees how both were obsessed with their enemies
without and their own truth within, we could almost
conclude that, if there is no adversity, certain creative
minds must invent it.

Creativity and Marginality

Of course, there are other ways of leaving paradise. Not all creativity takes place in a state of siege mentality. Yet, nearly always, there is some move away from the collective. In his book *Les Vrais Penseurs de Notre Temps*, Guy Sorman points out that one thing all the thinkers he interviewed had in common was that almost all had chosen to live in a country or place where they were "strangers," a long way from their original roots and belonging. They needed to feel themselves as marginal, as if the outer uprooting were a necessary counterpart to the inner exploration and creativity.[3]

In impossible love the marginalization takes place by virtue of the taboos and constrictions around its very existence. Separation from the safety of the group is not necessarily a choice made by the lovers, but one their love imposes on them, as Heloïse's did on her. She did not choose to leave her home and milieu; she was ostracized and persecuted by her uncle and his friends, and she had no choice but to flee. She did not choose the later separation from Abelard either. He decided, and she had little choice but to take the veil and cut herself even further off from the life and hopes she had left behind.

Still, Heloïse chose to be faithful to her love, and when she was thrown out of paradise, she espoused the consequences of her choice. In her way, she was a pioneer, and whatever her failings or failures, she did not become a martyr to love. Her vision was unwavering, and far from killing her, it kept her alive and well—intelligent, loyal, and creative to the end.

Creativity and marginality interact throughout the experience of an impossible love. Because of the obstacles to loving, there is no choice but to become more imaginative and resourceful than usual. As there is no support to be had from outside conditions or people, one must draw on undiscovered reserves within. Therefore, in the first flush of passion we may find ourselves re-inventing the world and not regretting the one we have left behind.

Then, as the darker aspects of passion appear, and the initial paradise gives way to suffering and difficulties, the creativity seems to disappear. We feel marginalized all right, but in vain. We have taken risks, forsaken our routines and social safety nets, and all for what? "Destructive" seems a better description of our impossible love than "creative."

These are difficult and even perilous moments to live through. If we get stuck in attributing the creative energy only to the love relationship and its potential viability, then indeed the creativity will disappear from our lives, leaving only bitterness in its wake. Just as we were lifted up, through no merit of our own, into passion's wonder, so have we been brought down, through no merit of our own, by its dark side. Such is the way of passion. We do not choose its course. We can only consent to follow.

We can, however, choose how we deal with its effects in our lives. If, like Heloïse, we can hold the painful tension of opposites and *be loyal both to the love and its impossibility in outer life*, then we may find that its very destructiveness has to do with something new in ourselves, a vision, an attitude, a new awareness we could never have learned in a book or in our ordinary human haunts.

In impossible love, sometimes we are Abelard, and sometimes Heloïse. Sometimes, like Abelard, we think we have found our place in life and are delighted with our own accomplishments, only to discover in the confusion of unexpected passion that everything we have done so far must be threatened or even lost, so that we can find out what our real accomplishment must be. Sometimes, like Heloïse, we have simply fit in comfortably until the passion of a hopeless love affair puts us in contact with an inner truth we must begin to serve. Often we can identify with both of them, loving the love and regretting the losses at the same time. In impossible love, we will always experience a loss of innocence about ourselves and the world and, with luck, a new creativity in that world. In order for this creativity to take place, however, there must be confrontation with the forbidden and numinous forces that erupt in passion and consent to the consequences that inevitably result from going where angels fear to tread. From the point of view of ordinary consciousness, this would appear suicidal and, indeed, in many ways it is. Yet, as we shall see, the greatness of the event can only yield its treasures if it is embraced fully in all its facettes.

PART II

Taboo and Hypocrisy:
Impossible Love—The Social Context

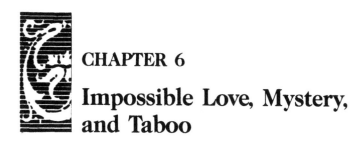

CHAPTER 6

Impossible Love, Mystery, and Taboo

Who Are the Abelards and Heloïses of Today?

What are these facettes? What are the conditions that make impossible love impossible, and what manner of people fall for its alluring impossibility? As I began work on the subject, it was clear from early on that the presence of taboos was intrinsic to this kind of love. They were obvious with Abelard and Heloïse, sub- tle in other cases. They were outer or inner, but they were there, irrefutable and indispensable.

Only when I began to tell people what I was writing about, however, did I become aware of par- ticular issues concerning the kind of individuals in- volved in these experiences. What struck me first was that one of two things invariably happened when I mentioned the expression "impossible love." Either my interlocutor looked blank and responded politely, a little embarrassed, "Oh, that's nice," or he or she lit up like a Christmas tree and exclaimed, "Oh, yes? I can't wait to read it, and I'd be happy to share my story if you need material!"

The ones who wanted to share had little in common with each other and did not at all correspond to any one type of individual I might have supposed vulnerable to impossible love. Yet, their emotional response was the same. Their faces changed; their eyes lit up with a blend of recognition and nostalgia.

After a while, I began guessing to myself which version someone would answer before they had even been asked the question. With time, I got quite good at this, making me realize how much our deepest psychological experiences put us into an unconscious bond with perfect strangers, while simultaneously making us seem like strangers to the people closest to us.

As the proliferation of growth groups, recovery groups, twelve-step groups, men's groups, and others attests, people need to feel themselves connected to each other through "kinship" bonds that are deeper than social or even familial ones—bonds that have more to do with meaning and inner experience than outer status or obligation. In this sense we are all heirs to the traditions of the Great Mystery Cults—be they Greek, Christian, Jewish, Masonic, or any other. In all mystery cults, certain individuals were chosen or allowed to undergo initiation into certain shared secrets. Their collective participation created a special bond among them and, through the sacred secret, a special relationship to the gods or goddesses presiding over the cult. Few of us today have the possibility of being officially initiated into such a cult, yet our psyches seek mystery and depths and find other means, unofficial ones, to accomplish the same thing.

The people who responded with such enthusiasm to the subject of impossible love knew what I was talking about. There was no need for explanation because they had been there. Willingly or unwillingly, they had been pulled into the mysterious darkness that seems so wrong on the surface, yet leaves such a mark that its "initiates" never forget, and do not usually want to. The people who did not respond very much probably had not been there. As Jean Duvignaud points out in his book *The Genesis of the Passions in Social Life*, not everyone is "a creature for [passionate] love."[1] In fact, he goes on, "the distribution of these cases does not, statistically, present any interest for sociologists who would rather leave a study of such anomalies to the tabloids or literature."[2] Impossible love is not for everyone. Other people may meet the depths in other ways, or possibly not at all. As to why life initiates us into one direction and not another, that remains a mystery as well. What is true of both groups, however, is that they look the same from the outside. Just as the participants in the Great Mysteries of pagan times were ordinary people from all walks of life, indistinguishable in appearance and manner from the non-participants, so is it for most people who have undergone a major inner experience. From the outside it rarely shows.

The stories I have heard and read and studied in order to write this book belong for the most part to ordinary individuals. They are the stories of friends, analysands, strangers, and acquaintances. Some, as with Abelard and Heloïse, belong to the past; some belong to individuals in fiction and film, but even there these are not the stories of madmen or kings, but of ordinary people doing everyday things, at least on the outside. None of the examples are taken from people who were more neurotic or needy or misadapted than most normal modern individuals. None was looking frantically for love and relationship.

These lovers were doctors, social workers, psychologists, film makers, academics, members of Parliament, office workers, and business people getting on with their lives when "it" hit. As the member of Parliament said, "it was the split second experience that changes everything, the car smash, the letter we shouldn't have opened, the lump in the breast or groin, the blinding flash."[3] Love at the wrong time in the wrong place and with the wrong person. Impossible love. Unexpected, unwelcome, and irresistible.

Of course, not every "fall" takes place so quickly and dramatically. It isn't always love at first sight. Sometimes the protagonists have known each other quite a while before something, suddenly, clicks. Whatever the timing, however, the first spontaneous reaction on the part of the lover or lovers is usually "Oh no, not this, not him/her, not now!" A sense of enormous dread collides with a sense of enormous elation. Both will prove to be founded. Everything is both absolutely right and terribly wrong. Right because of the wonder it ushers in, wrong because it cannot and should not be.

Some will say "yes" to this encounter with impossible love but will emerge from the experience embittered and full of regret. They will try to forget the whole thing and "get back to normal" as soon as possible. They will seek ways to explain or rationalize the error of their own ways and will likely not consider their experience of such "wrong" loving as a trans-formative moment in their lives. In fact, their lives may have been changed a great deal or very little. It doesn't really matter. Since there is no inner value given to the drama, it turns into a piece of psychologi-cal "junk," relegated to the closet of shameful secrets and best-forgotten memories. These embittered lovers would identify more with Abelard than Heloïse, though even Abelard, despite his protestations, had the courage to live and create out of the consequences of his passion. In spite of himself, he became more than he had been. This is not always the case. Some-times it is possible to erase the evidence and go on as before.

For obvious reasons, I did not come into contact with very many of the individuals who didn't value their impossible loves. For them there is no story to tell, just a secret to keep, and I was not interested in prying into other people's closets. What I cared about was being open to the stories that came to me, through both chance and invitation. The result is that there are more voices of Heloïse than Abelard in my de-scriptions, Heloïses of both sexes who had lived an impossible love and knew that it meant something important in their lives. Sometimes they knew this only vaguely and wanted to find out more; sometimes they could articulate their story with great clarity and insight.

Always, whether closer to Abelard or Heloïse, our modern lovers confronted outer taboos as well as inner resistances in order to live out their love affair. As we shall see, in fact, the inner and outer taboos are indispensable. Stolen waters are indeed sweeter, and the taboos do heighten the intensity of the passion. But even more important, the transgression of taboos isolates and ostracizes the individual, forcing him or her into a major questioning of old values and a possibly new and more individual direction.

Taboos: Fear and Trembling

It may seem surprising, in our enlightened age, to speak of taboos. We easily accept that, in the time of Heloïse and Abelard, the so-called Dark Ages, taboos were still part of social reality. But we rarely stop to realize that we too live in an age of taboos. We are no longer subject to the rigidity of a feudal system and the absolute authority of a dogmatic Church, but our society, like all societies, has its way of making certain things sacred and others profane. Not only do we have taboos, but we need them, for without taboos there is chaos.

Expressed in a "complex *symbolic* system, taboos define boundaries and limits in religious and social areas."[4] As such, they reflect not how we interact as citizens in a state concerned with law and order, but how we inter-connect as human beings in an age-old web of barely conscious fears and hopes. We obey the law in order not to pay a fine or go to jail, but we obey taboos in order not to be expelled from the social community we live in. Taboos reach down into our collective psyche and define our very humanity. Some are universal—the incest taboo, for example. Others are more limited to specific times and cultures—food or fashion taboos, for example. In either case, violating them may bring immediate ostracism and loss of membership from the human group that holds them.

This seems extreme, but taboos are about extremes. They are always found around the weakest and the strongest points in a social fabric, the ones to be controlled and the ones to be protected. They establish zones of untouchability around these troublesome or vital areas in order to preserve social stability. The strongest and highest values might be represented by a king, a special sanctuary, or a sacred object which must be protected at all costs, as it symbolizes the essence of the culture's identity. A law would not be enough to render these things untouchable. Only a taboo, making them sacred, creates the fear and trembling that guarantees their immunity.

As for the lowest or weakest points in the social hierarchy, they must be controlled at all costs—else they break loose and threaten the highest. Sex and other instinctual drives and appetites have always been favorite targets of taboo in most cultures. Labeling them demonic has more effect than just calling them illegal.

Whether taboos concern the sacred or the unholy, they remind us that, even in our age of "anything goes," we are human beings, and we are terrified of chaos. Total loss of control or stability remains as frightening for the community as it is for the individual, and we have a natural tendency to establish and maintain consensus on some areas that absolutely cannot be challenged or infringed upon.

In our contemporary Western culture, where God has been declared dead and the devil has been roasted in Hollywood, what could these areas be? In a world where nothing seems sacred anymore—neither flag, nor king, nor God himself—where are these strongest points, the highest values around which there might still be taboos? And in a society that condones Madonna masturbating in public and Schwarzenegger terminating his enemies in a blaze of gore, are there really any "weak" points considered dangerous enough to still merit the application of a taboo? Indeed, traditional taboos have weakened so much, it is difficult to see where they still exist, if at all. In the area of love, one way of locating some would be to update the story of Abelard and Heloïse and relate it to some impartial average citizens, asking for their reaction. A few examples of possible responses might go as follows:

"What, he used his role of teacher and person in a position of trust to abuse her sexually?!"

"What, she spent her *whole life* waiting for a man to answer her letters?"

"What, he had the gall to publish *his* version of their story, when he was to blame for it all in the first place?"

"Oh, that's just one more story of erotic obsession. Have you read the book *Damage*?"

Under the surface, in apparently anodyne com-
ments, the taboos are there. Taboos against women
loving "too much" or living for men, against men talking about *their* experiences with women, against love
in any form that is not politically correct and caring,
and especially against real passion which is quickly
turned into "just sex." The difference between today's
taboos and those of the past is that they are less obvious, and there is less universal consensus around
them.

Since we no longer have a close-knit homoge-
neous tribal society that defines our common values
and humanity, we attach ourselves to sub-cultures to
find a sense of collective belonging, and these sub-
cultures create their own rating system of highest and
lowest, best and worst. Under subtle or less subtle
guises, they determine what is thinkable and what is
not, what are the untouchable values and what are
the forbidden zones. Contrary to the advertisements
of American Express, membership does not just mean
privilege. It also means taboos. Political correctness
is just a new version of an old need. What was once
decreed by Church and Royalty is now in the hands
of various political, corporate, and professional groups.
You need not belong to a right-wing faction to come
under the influence of taboos. The most officially pro-
gressive movements, including psychology, feminism,
and ecology, generate their own "indexes" of forbidden thoughts and acts.

In Jungian psychology, for example, it was taboo
for years to refer to Freudian psychology as anything
but retrograde and reductive. On the other side, ortho-

dox Freudians protected *their* church by making it taboo to refer to Jung as anything but an irrational mystic who lost touch with reality when he broke with Freud and left the fold of the true believers. With time, members of each group have come to see not just the merit, but even the necessity, of integrating different aspects of the other's psychology. But the taboos do not disappear, they just change places. Professional or social communities will always protect their identity by defining what is in or out, what can be questioned and what cannot.

On a larger scale, these groups and all of us, in or out of them, are influenced by recent changes in collective values brought about by the emergence of new voices in the public arena. Ecology, feminism, and psychology, for example, propose consciousness-raising and new freedoms, but paradoxically they create norms and untouchable truths of their own. In their most popularized and simplistic forms, some of these truths emerge as follows:

> Green is good, women are good, whales are good, children are good.

> Most industry is bad, most men are bad, except the ones we know who aren't and who are our best friends.

> Sex is fine and healthy if it takes place between two consenting adults who have read the right manuals or if you are a famous movie star who makes millions doing it in front of a camera.

It is not fine or healthy to do it inexpertly or to do it in front of a camera when you are not famous and just barely make a living out of it.

It is not good to have none at all.

Love is very good as long as it is caring, supportive, and understanding, but not if there is any hint of power, competition or indifference. Then it isn't love anyway.

Admittedly, I've exaggerated some of the above for effect. Still, I think if you watch enough television and read enough popular middle-class magazines, you will probably find examples of just such judgments. For several months in the winter season of 1993, major American television networks ran Sunday night "specials" dramatizing the subjects of dead-beat fathers and their forgotten children, unrequited male lovers turning into murderous stalkers, and middle-class husbands subjecting their wives and children to torture and cruelty behind the closed doors of suburban paradise. Certainly, much of this really happens. Certainly, it is crucial to open our eyes on reality and denounce such abuse. But do we really denounce this abominable behavior by making such relentlessly stereotypical, sensationalist depictions of it, or do we just reinforce our need to see the world in good and bad colors? It is difficult to turn off the television set after watching such horrors and to remember that, as a rule, both men and women are more complex than the characters portrayed there.

If nothing else, however, these over-simplified modern versions of good and bad do reflect our need for psychological certainties involving the limits and boundaries that are not addressed by the outer political and legal codes. Where old taboos fall or fail, we will create others, and we need to do so in order to feel ourselves connected to a social and spiritual anchor.

Sometimes, however, it is important to break taboos in order to create a new order. Every revolution starts by breaking a taboo. Off with the king's head or down with sexual puritanism—either one signals the end and transgression of a taboo. These were collective movements whose time had come. The old taboos were no longer meaningful to the culture in which they had taken root. Breaking them, however, nearly always brings about as much destruction as construction. The French Revolution, which demolished the taboos encircling the Divine Right of Kings, was extremely bloody in its reality and extremely creative in the ideas it put into the world. To a greater or lesser extent, this is true of most revolutions, whether they be political, or scientific, or social.

Taboos around Love

It is also true in individual revolutions. Whenever we break our own inner taboos, or those of the milieu we belong to, we can expect to harvest a maelstrom of both creative and destructive energies. When Abelard and Heloïse scorned the taboos of the society in which they lived, they found themselves in the eye of a storm which did not abate until they were separated and in exile. Our modern lovers, caught in the passion of impossible love and as yet unburied and unreunited by the forgiving hand of history, will experience a similar turbulence in the forces they release. We seem a long way from the social strait-jacket and double standard of twelfth-century Europe. Yet we have our own ideas about "appropriate" and "inappropriate" love. Like any society that ever existed, we have at least implicit rules governing who can love whom, when, and how, and these rules still concern issues of power and gender, just as they always have.

For example, it is all right for an older heterosex-ual man to love a much younger heterosexual woman, but when an older gay man proclaims his attachment for a much younger man, we are likely to think "lust" when he speaks of "love." As for an older woman who would love a much younger man or woman, we prob-ably substitute "mother instinct" for what she so naively calls love. To continue along this line, a black man who loves a white woman may secretly be thought to just use her as symbol of his macho vic-tory over white men, while the woman must be so hard up she can only find a mate by leaving her own racial group. A teacher who falls in love with a stu-dent must be in the grip of a mid-life crisis, and the student who loves a teacher can only be looking for a parental substitute. A therapist who falls in love with a patient must be blinded by personal problems not sufficiently addressed in his or her own therapy, while the patient who would enter into a love affair with the doctor therapist can only be the victim of his or her own transference and the abuse of power by the helper. We may sentimentally subscribe to the adage that "love conquers all," but when this love appears in unexpected or unlikely places, we are quick to turn it into something else.

If we look to one of the more "classical" places for love to be in the wrong place, we might still find examples in adultery, for society and spouses still do not take lightly the betrayal and rupture within the established couple. As studies and polls constantly remind us, at least half of all people in married or stable relationships do have outside affairs; however, today such goings-on do not necessarily cause separation and tragedy, especially when "just sex" is involved. And even though more than a third of marriages and relationships end in divorce and separation, and many of the partners will establish another relationship soon after, this is serial monogamy, not passion. It is more a result of our consumer society mentality that proposes exchanging the old model for the new than a result of passion's passage.

No, we have to look for something more in the "wrongness" of a love affair for it to be powerful enough to foster and define a passion that breaks with the past and collides with social taboos. Adultery, as infidelity, just isn't enough anymore, not in most circles anyway. It must first of all be adultery with love, for love of another person threatens the marriage far more than sex. Sexual infidelity may mean betrayal, but not necessarily rupture. Second of all, the love must be with a member of a taboo group, a person too close or too far to be considered an appropriate object of loving. A close friend of the couple, a trusted confidant, a grown-up step-daughter, or a person of another race, another generation, another milieu, another class, another sexual persuasion. Whether impossible love breaks into a marriage or into the life of a person otherwise "free," it will bring something radically different and threatening to the status quo.

In this sense love is far more subversive than sex. Marriage may be regulated, sexuality may be controlled, but love does not obey commands. It happens or it doesn't. It can be judged and condemned and forbidden, but the love itself cannot be taken away from the lovers, unless they themselves deny it. In the tragic love stories that we remember, it is the fidelity of the lovers to their love, in spite of the taboos and the impossibility, that moves us so. In story after story, the lovers have no regrets. They loved, lived a brief moment of paradise on earth, and then were separated and lost everything, including, on occasion, their lives. But there is no longing for the old life or for return to the group they belonged to before they transgressed.

Heloïse on her death bed in the convent proclaims she is still the spouse of Abelard more than the bride of Christ. Francesca, a Florentine nobleman's wife, who was relegated to hell for her adulterous affair with Paolo, tells Dante in The Divine Comedy that she has no regrets. Though the lovers cannot even speak together in the hell they share, she still loves Paolo and would rather be there than alone in heaven. The hero of the book Damage confides to a friend near the end when all is lost,

"My wife wished that I'd died. Not lived to do this."

The friend replies, "But then you'd never have lived at all, would you?"

Hero: "No."

Friend: "So be it. Few regret the experience. Be grateful you made the journey. Few people do. Perhaps it's just as well. Tragedy almost always follows."[5]

Love, Transgression, Tragedy, and yet no regrets. These make for a potent combination in the life of an individual. The "no regrets" eliminates the possibility of hypocrisy, of pretending it was all a big mistake or didn't really count. It means that there *was* a revolution. In one life, or in many, and that no cover-up or opposition can put back the clock and make everything the way it was before. As Francesco Alberoni says in *The In-Love Shock*, "Love is a revolution, it separates what was united, and unites what was separated."[6] The lovers separate from their milieu and their own inner convictions in order to unite with each other, and in doing so they cause changes around them.

When the love is very passionate and very impossible, the changes may be radical and destructive, causing division and strife where there was harmony and consensus. These lovers turn into revolutionaries in spite of themselves, as they confront the culture they belong to and live in with questions about its own deepest taboos. Stories of impossible inter-racial love, for example, often do far more to make us question our own unconscious assumptions than all the official speeches on the importance of not being racist. This is why love is more subversive than sex, and why an impossible love differs from what we would call a purely erotic obsession. It is also why we as a culture persistently try to put all passion under the label of "just" an erotic obsession.

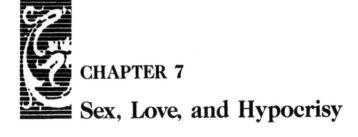

CHAPTER 7

Sex, Love, and Hypocrisy

It's "Just" Sex

Sex is everywhere. Television, books, movies all treat us to a regular dose of unbridled sex as entertainment, and for the most part this is considered a healthy, if sometimes uncomfortable, part of the sexual revolution. Whether the characters are total strangers who will never see each other again or passionate partners in a great love story, their affair is neatly summed up by such expressions as sexual obsession, erotic possession, etc.

Sexual abuse comes in as the other side of our fascination with sex. Whatever the psychological drama or trauma involved, we want to know the details. What really happened? Meaning, generally, what did *he* do to *her* physically? Rarely do we hear in such detail about blatant abuse of power in other areas. Browbeating by bosses, silent treatments by spouses, nagging by parents, exploitation by employees. Rarely, for that matter, in actual journalism or in entertainment do we read headlines about Love. It wouldn't sell.

Since "just" sex supposedly does not involve our

hearts, we can distance ourselves from it and put its ravages down to our Western problem with instincts, patriarchy, or hormones gone wild, as we follow the sensational details. It is far too powerful a force to be allowed to run rampant, but there are ways to monitor and control it, and every society has produced them. Laws can be passed and punishments fixed for individuals who commit sexual crimes. Programs and theories can be applied to victims of sexual obsession. Manuals can be published about sexual techniques. The law, psychology, and science can deal with sex, at least on paper.

But what heart can be contained by the law or explained by science? You can get a degree in sexology, but not in love. It is easier to reduce passion to its purely physical components than to admit its disruptive force in our psyches.

Equating an impossible love with sexual madness is all the more tempting, in that the two frequently take place in the same forbidden sphere. Both go against convention, and even against taboos, in regard to the right kind of love object. The difference lies in the hypocrisy that surrounds sexual transgression, which makes it easier to identify and integrate into the collectivity than love.

What few taboos still regulate sex can be gotten around through the loopholes in the system, for even if certain sexual behaviors are officially condemned as undesirable, they are also unofficially recognized as inevitable. Why else would prostitution and pornography be both illegal and constantly available? These more or less clandestine activities are part of the normal deviations that every society builds into its codes. As Duvignaud says in *The Genesis of the Passions in Social Life*, such hypocrisy is "absolutely necessary for cultural stability because it permits a clandestine pursuit of pleasure and happiness that is neither a threat nor an open challenge to the official ideology."[1] The message is not "Don't ever do it," but "If you must do it, don't get caught," and, if you do get caught, as in the case of certain American politicians surprised with the wrong paramour, then you can control the damage by making a public statement of remorse and regret for succumbing to such temptation.

Even sexual abuse has until recently been part of the system, and what is surprising is not that this is so, but that we are finally beginning to denounce it. For sexual abuse has always existed. Why have we taken so long to discover it? Because the taboos surrounding people in power protected them and made them untouchable. Theoretically, for example, it was taboo to commit incest, but this taboo could be ignored in favor of another—the taboos regarding the omniscience of the patriarch. If there is conflict, taboos around the highest values come before those around the lowest. The weakest (women and children) needed to be controlled; the strongest (men) needed to be untouchable. Social stability depended on a fixed hierarchy of power.

As a result, it could be admissible even for the most admired leaders to have moments of weakness, as long as these could be dealt with within the system and its loopholes. Jack Kennedy had his Marilyn, the

TABOO AND HYPOCRISY

president relaxed, the presidency was not in danger. Others in positions of power, public or private, have had their mistresses and their dips into pornography. Still others have systematically sexually abused those weaker than they, including their own children, proving that the incest taboo has been less weighty, until recently, than the taboo involving the untouchable father figure.

This untouchability, of course, is exactly what has been challenged in recent times, first by feminists and now by groups of the general population. It is changing so fast, in fact, that we are almost witnessing an "enantiodromia," a conversion to the opposite. The patriarch, the untouchable of yesteryear, becomes the pariah of today.

With these changes, new hypocrisies will accompany the development of new taboos. Already, we are seeing the taboo around women's shadows—their capacity to be abusive and villainous. According to the media, women can do no wrong unless they are pulled into it by men or are exceptionally and demonically evil. Otherwise, they are only good, only victims, and in order to reinforce this myth, we must resort to good old hypocrisy, which allows for women to privately and secretly act out their all too human vices, but not to admit them as part of their collective identity and complexity.

Hypocrisy versus the Value of Love

When we return to the area of impossible love, we find that hypocrisy is much harder to maintain here for both sexes, no matter what the taboos in fashion. There are no loopholes through which to live impossible love just a little bit from time to time. There is no public scene of remorse and regret to look forward to. Like a sexual obsession or acting out, impossible love may be hidden and wrong, but unlike the sexual deviation, it is not experienced as something dirty to apologize for or something criminal to run from. Its very value as lived by the lovers is what makes it problematical for society.

If Kennedy had fallen in love with Marilyn, it could have caused a much greater disturbance to his functions than having an affair with her did. How would we have felt about seeing Marilyn at his side instead of Jackie, representing the country abroad at State dinners and in the White House? Probably not happy at all. She was too vulgar, too sexy, too silly to be an appropriate partner, and though we find it feasible that he would want to sleep with her, we would not like to think he could love her. That would have changed our whole image of the man, not to speak of the aura around Camelot. Wrong love has changed the course of history more often than wrong sex. Despite our obsession with romance and delight in tales of lovers who braved all to be together, when it is closer to home we want love to stay within the bounds of permitted emotional attachment.

Who decides what "wrong" is? Our milieu does, we do. As we have seen, as members of a group we all have a vested interest in maintaining its stability and cohesion by judging what and who may be admitted. We introduce a new lover to our friends with fear and trembling, knowing perfectly well that their reactions will have a considerable effect on our future relationship and even on our feelings for that person. We suffer for our friends and even feel alienated from them when they are involved with someone who does not fit with the group, who seems "not good enough" for our friend or too impossible for a relationship with that person to bode for happiness and harmony.

For example, when a good friend of mine, a therapist herself, told me she was in love with one of her patients, I spent weeks worrying about her. I was sure she would not be loved by him equally. After all, I said to myself, everyone knows that patients cannot love. They only have transferences. I was also sure she was running the risk of losing her license and reputation for transgressing the modern-day taboo of such relationships. Much to my own surprise, I found myself in the role of the Super-Ego, the voice of social conscience, and tried gently but firmly to open her eyes to the consequences of her folly.

Fortunately, she did not listen to me or my Super-Ego. She believed what her heart told her. Their love, in spite of appearances, became a possible one, with none of the devastating consequences of a wrongly placed passion that I had anticipated.

Her case is unusual. We would have to surmise that for her the inner taboo of not following her heart was even stronger than the outer one of following it to the wrong place. What is more, her lover felt exactly the same way. Unlike Abelard and Heloïse, neither felt that the outer taboos, in her profession or his own personal situation, carried a comparable weight to the simple injunction to love and be together. There were obstacles and difficulties to be sure, but the combined weight of their mutual conviction didn't give the obstacles a chance to create an insurmountable conflict.

In the situation of impossible love, there is a different distribution of taboo and desire, love and fear. They become equal weights pulling in opposite directions and leading to an impasse that has no satisfactory resolution in one direction or the other. Another story of a woman professional who fell in love with a client illustrates this sad truth. Unlike my friend above, this woman, let us call her Susan, was not only an active professional woman, a lawyer in her case, but also a prominent leader in a local firm. She had worked for years to help found and put this firm on its feet, and until she fell in love, it was close to being the most important thing in her life. She had been married, divorced, had brought up three children, and practiced law working for others, but the firm had been her real "baby"—the source of her creative energy and efforts.

The woman client, "Nell," with whom she fell in love, worked for a large financial institution and was in a long-standing relationship with another woman. She had always been discreet about her personal life, neither hiding nor flaunting her unconventional choice. When she and Susan met for the first time at Susan's office, business, not love, was on their minds. Their working agenda completed, they talked on into the evening. "Business" lunches followed, and passion was born, much to each woman's surprise. Like two Abelards, they both had a great deal to lose by consenting to live out such an impossible love. Like two Heloïses, they fully consented, nevertheless, to follow their hearts instead of their minds. So it seemed, anyway.

With time it became clear that neither could rise above her fears to lead the other out of their impasse. Nell, who was ready to put her present relationship in jeopardy, was unable to stand the idea of Susan being the object of scandal in her profession. Susan, who was willing to take such a risk, could not bear to be the "other woman," responsible for the breakup of Nell's household. Like Abelard and Heloïse, "They wept for each other's misfortunes" and came up against their own deep taboos. Each could accept the possibility of destruction in her own world, neither could accept to be the agent of destruction in the world of the other.

Like any lovers, they needed to idealize each other. It was impossible to love and at the same time cause the downfall of their ideal. This was exactly the dilemma that got Abelard and Heloïse into trouble. She was willing to lose her reputation, but could not bear to make him lose his status of Great Philosopher and Scholar by marrying her. As for Abelard, needing to idealize Heloïse and keep her in the role of Perfect Woman-Mother-Saint, he could not acknowledge her letters as a lover because that would have been to acknowledge his own part in taking her off the pedestal in the first place.

We find similar tensions between desire and ideal in all impossible love—"I want you, I'll do anything to have you, including put my life and reputation on the line, and I want you to do the same. But at the same time, I don't want you to do the same because then you would be at my feet and no longer ideal."

The very obstacles to our loving, the marriage, the professional reputation, the difference in age, or race, or class, or nationality, are the same ones that dazzle us into making the Other into an ideal. These differences and obstacles belong to another world, a world we do not usually participate in. We resent them and are ill at ease with them—why do you have to be married, or so much younger, or in a city so far away—and yet we are irresistibly attracted to them. They are as necessary as they are unwelcome.

The necessity, though, is not on a conscious level. The only necessity we are immediately aware of is the need to be with the Other, to be able to love freely. We are so busy trying to cope with the wonder and power of our feelings and the conflicts they provoke that we don't realize that our psyches are setting us up for a plunge into *its* idea of necessity, not our own. In fact, consciously, our first reaction will often be "Who needs this now?" Clearly, from the ego's point of view, nobody. It knows there is trouble ahead.

Given the trouble, the tensions, the taboos, and the conflicts of values and worlds, why do we say yes? Are we just the victims of our own weakness, or is there something more that pulls us in, willingly and irrevocably?

PART III

Intimations of Immortality:
Impossible Love and Religious Experience

CHAPTER 8
The Light Above

Chosen for Great Things

In the beginning of the book I referred to the "unknown depths" that lure us into the magic of an impossible love story. It could be added that, in both
legend and actual experience, the unknown depths
contain unknown heights as well, and neither is mundane. We go from a blaze of light to a tunnel of
darkness, aware that we are partaking in something
extra-ordinary in both spheres and helpless to prevent
it, even if we wanted to.

In terms of analytical psychology, we have become possessed by an archetype. In other words, we
have been carried away by energies of the unconscious
that transcend our usual capacities and perceptions.
Paradoxically, what we feel as the most intensely personal and individual moments are made possible by
the most impersonal forces.

At first, these forces make us feel like gods, chosen
for great things. Unaware of their presence and encouraged by their seductive promises, we identify with
their power and enter into a state of psychological in-

flation that fills us with the hot air of our recent elevation into love. What we do not foresee in this ecstatic state is that the very forces that took us up will bring us down again, for that is the very nature of archetypal possession. C. G. Jung's cogent definition of such a state describes its dangers well. In speaking of "inflation," he says that it occurs "when an archetypal content seizes hold of the psyche with a kind of primal force and compels it to *transgress the bounds of humanity.* The consequence is a puffed-up attitude, loss of free will, delusion and enthusiasm for good and evil alike."[1]

In the words "transgress the bounds of humanity" we hear an echo of the foregoing discussion of taboos, and the relationship between taboo and archetype emerges, making us realize that going against taboos never takes place in an ordinary state of mind. Both social and individual revolutions take their initial psychic energy from the "primal force" of unconscious energies that alter the minds of their perpetrators. Excess and exaggeration are the hallmarks of any radical change. Otherwise, the movement could not gather enough momentum to win over the habits and barriers of the past.

At the same time, for the people involved, this excess leads not only to extremes but, as Jung says, to loss of free will and even to delusion. The madness of the in-love state makes it impossible to discern between real and unreal, good or bad. We are in another world with its own geography and measures.

The Heights

In the beginning phase especially, it feels as if the forces that have elected us into the company of the gods are all on our side. We have been taken out of our usual world and transported to a planet where all is exceptional, significant, grandiose. As in any love affair, we revel in the discovery of the Oneness and the Totality that a beginning love creates. We are no longer alone and incomplete. We float in the illusion of inner unity, of being known and knowing an Other totally, of communication and understanding without effort or barrier, of care and solidarity and utter loyalty at last. The pleasure of this togetherness and symbiosis is all the greater in that we live and work in a world so obsessed with autonomy and heroic individualism.

Naturally, in the normal course of events and in the case of possible love, these illusions will slowly give way as the two partners get to know each other and no longer just idealize each other. Their love will become less ideal, more human, less absolute, and more nuanced. In impossible love such changes will not take place. Instead of coming down to earth, the lovers will go farther and farther away from it. As the archetypal forces substitute for the shocks of reality, the ideals will grow stronger and the absolutes as well. There will be no nuances.

On the other hand, there will be a feeling of Involvement in a Great Work, a Meaningful Process, that transcends ordinary reality. As Milan Kundera says in his book *Immortality*, because the passion is impossible to integrate into everyday life, it brings about a sense of participating in something that must be worked out on an "other worldly level,"[2] and this challenge replaces the usual details, negotiations, and explorations of a possible love. Living on this other-worldly and archetypal level, then, produces an intensity and urgency that seemingly go in the direction of the Loved one, but that, in fact, go in the direction of a mystic experience. Suddenly we are involved with Superior Events, with Greatness, and with God. We feel elated and heroic, in touch with our own inner god-like essence and that of the other person. In impossible love we begin to have intimations of immortality.

A woman relates, "I felt we could re-invent the world. We met on every level, emotionally, intellectually, sexually, totally, and so there seemed there was nothing we couldn't have done together. The miracle of our passion seemed to justify all the pain and destruction it was wreaking in our lives and around us. It was like the 'self-verifying' experiences that the Church used to refer to. The experience of grace that could never be explained or communicated or analyzed. It just was and it justified everything." With a degree in theology and a university chair, she knew what she was talking about when she referred to the Church. In her case, the passion she lived with a married doctor nearly ruined both of their careers. It also put her in touch for the first time with what she had been teaching, i.e., the religious experience.

In another example from the book *Damage*, the

hero describes the moment of passion's epiphany in his life in similar terms:

> A stillness descended upon me. I sighed a deep sigh, as if I had suddenly slipped out of a skin. I felt old and content. The shock of recognition had passed through my body like a powerful current. *Just for a moment I had met my sort, another of my species.* [emphasis mine] I would be grateful for that and would let it slip away. *I had been home.* For a moment, but longer than most people. It was enough, once, for a lifetime.[3]

In fact, it was not enough. His naive prediction that life would go on as before was coming from the voice of his still reasonable ego. Soon after, he would embark on the road to total destruction in a passionate affair with that person of his "sort and species."

The speaker, an MP in Britain who has fallen in love with his son's fiancée, continues later to speak in terms of transcendence, even as his outer life crumbles around him. He speaks of "being brought into being by another . . . to create our own universes" and of "going to the outer reaches of my being,"[4] and toward the end he says, "in the center of my crown, like a diamond, rested the only truth that mattered to me—Anna."[5]

From him, as from others, we have allusions to god-like creativity, absolute truth, omnipotent certitude, and that something exceptional that justifies everything. In another story, a university professor in his forties falls fatally in love with a pupil of seventeen, and when his wife asks him what has happened to make him leave her, his job, and all he has worked for, he can only answer, "I have met an exceptional being."[6] It is the call of the exceptional, to that "something else" beyond our usual limited human scope that pulls us in further and further. In a world of routine and conformity, we feel Chosen, and like Moses we are ready to cross our own Red Sea of passion and pain to heed the call from heaven.

Like Heloïse, we find ourselves possessed of new resolution and determination and strength in the face of adversity. We will brave not only the outer obstacles and inner fears, but also our lovers themselves if they prove, like Abelard, to be resistant to our élan. A man writes to his lover in a far-off country at the bitter end of their impossible love, "I would have been there for you whether you had become crippled, bankrupt or crazy." A woman writing to the forbidden and elusive lover in her life writes, "I loved the hero, the tender poet, the tin man and the bastard too." The psychological inflation fed by the challenges and difficulties in impossible love makes heroes and heroines of us all. There is so little to build on outside that we become architects of our own greatness within.

Necessity and Treachery of the High

Viewed objectively, these statements can be seen as grandiose or inflated, even histrionic. This, however, is how any experience beyond the ordinary makes us feel. A great business deal, a great success in any area, a moment between people when everything "clicks" and we feel on "top of the world."

Usually these moments do not last. Life takes care of bringing us back to earth and our ordinary state of mind. Sometimes, however, in order to prolong these special states, we may resort to artificial means: drugs, alcohol, gambling—and other addictions that give us the rush and make us feel "divine." Humans have always used substances to alter their states of mind and consciousness. They have used them in order to feel no pain, to amplify their creativity and perceptions, to join with others in rituals of *"participation mystique"* and collective symbiosis, and above all to be in contact with a transcendental power and energy.[7]

The search for the "high" is universal. There would be no spirituality, no invention, no new discoveries, no adventure in human life without experiences of being high. The trouble with such altered states of consciousness, however, is that it is hard to control them. As we have seen, once in the grip of an archetype we lose the faculty of free choice and will. Other cultures recognized that such states were mostly dangerous and only occasionally desirable, and they surrounded the taking of drugs or other mind-changing techniques with rituals in order to contain and channel their effects.

Today we have few rituals to do this, and so the highs open the doors as much to the demons as to the gods in our psyches. In a *grande passion*, something similar happens. When we consent to it, we open the door to enormous forces that make us feel in touch with both the gods and the demons. All is bigger than life itself—our desire, our strength, our certitude, our vision, our capacity for infinite love. But all is bigger on the negative side as well—our pain, our fears, our doubts, and even our capacity for infinite hate. The lure of immortality can also turn into what seems like eternal damnation.

CHAPTER 9

The Darkness Below

The Depths

The feeling of being damned instead of blessed is just the opposite side of the psychological inflation. In either event we feel chosen for something special: in one case the light, in the other the darkness. The difference is that we never questioned the delightful effects of the positive side. They may have seemed miraculous or unexpected, but somehow they also seemed so right, considering who we are and what we have gone through in our lives. It is only when the darkness falls in impossible love that we begin to wonder if we are not the victims of something greater than our own merit or mistakes would warrant. As paradise turns into hell, we realize that we are not as in control and in harmony with the universe as we thought. Whether we know it or not consciously, the fact is that the archetype is in charge and has been from the beginning.

At this point we might gladly forsake paradise in order to leave hell and get back to the safety and dullness of good old earth. But this is rarely possible.

More often, once we have bought the ticket, we have to go on the whole trip. Light and dark, high and low, with only exhaustion in between. As Adolf Guggenbühl-Craig said in an essay on shadow, "One of the great tasks of the individuation process is to experience the dark destructive side,"[1] and if this is true, then an impossible love must be one of the surer ways to get on the road to individuation.

Generally, the dark destructive energy in our lives is held in abeyance by our consciousness and good manners. Like the high that requires an altered state of consciousness, the low comes out more in moments of stress or inflation, when consciousness is vulnerable to unconscious archetypal energies. Negative feelings come to the surface and force us to confront what we would like to avoid. Truths about ourselves, truths about the Other. Most of all, perhaps, truths about life that violate our innocence and illusions. *Yet in impossible love, as in any important emotional event, if we avoided the darkness, we would just accomplish half the work, miss its deepest meaning, and, like Parsifal, have to start all over again— probably by repeating another impossible love.*

Lovers in the Depths

In fairy tales and legends, the opposites of light and shadow are usually lived in sequence as outer realities. First the lovers, together in perfect bliss, live their paradise on earth. They then are separated to a long purgatory of exile and longing on earth, or condemned and sent straight away to hell. In actual life, however, most protagonists of an impossible love live their heaven and hell within seconds of each other, in a constant alternation between hope and despair.

In a passage from the book *Changing Heaven*, we read of a married man and his unmarried lover driving through a snow storm, on their way to their secret first rendezvous. Alone at last. Time is short, but theirs; the world is put on hold as they enter into their Eternity of a few hours together. Then, blithely, he begins to make small talk, about his other life, the new dog he and his wife bought for the children, the children's progress at school, the dinner they will all prepare for guests on Saturday night. In this instant, for her, paradise turns into hell as these "simple statements hit her with the impact of an ax."[2] Hurt by his insensitivity, she is also shocked by the realization of her own feelings of great jealousy and reflects to herself with great foreboding, "until now this has been a summer road for her."[3]

Her spontaneous reflection on the change of seasons in the very landscape outside reflects the essence of the darkness and change she will live throughout their affair. The impact of the ax is the impact of a splitting, the end of the illusion of wholeness she had about her love or her own life. Though she returns after their tryst to her own space, an apartment "where it has been so easy to keep the world out,"[4] her psychic virginity has been lost for good. Her passion tears her out of the genteel schoolteacher world of literature, where she has lived through other people's stories, and into the center of her own drama.

Since her lover is so elusive and secretive, she has fewer of the moments of bliss we alluded to in the previous chapter and more of the moments of pain. Her passion is a "bad trip" with more shadow than light and, for this reason, is a particularly good illustration of the kind of hell that all lovers eventually fall into in an impossible love.

The "summer road" turns into a winter one. The lovers go from the tropical heat of desire and fusion into the arctic cold of misunderstanding and separation. Work, familiar routine, and lukewarm, safe houses of friends no longer offer any comfort as the lovers ricochet back and forth between the equator and the antipodes. Not only the temperature goes through violent changes, but also our very sense of space. One moment all is huge; our hearts, our love, our souls, our minds expand to contain the entire universe. Nothing is too petty to include. Like the poet Whitman, we "contain multitudes."

Then, in other moments, it all retracts. We cannot share our life with that of our lover and feel a prisoner of tiny moments and tiny rooms. As the heroine of *Changing Heaven* relates, "The [hotel] rooms' borders are the limits of her existence,"[5] and each time they see each other in this stolen time and rented space, "she is already waiting for the next time."[6] There is never enough time, never enough space—out there. And so the time and space grow greater within, and the passion takes up more and more room as it turns into obsession.

At that point we enter into a region "where no help is possible."[7] What better description of hell? The trouble is, we didn't see the warning sign, "Abandon all hope ye who enter." We thought we were in heaven, on the summer road, when we initially said yes to the voyage. We did not bargain for the other side—the sleepless nights, the pain, the humiliation of participating in something so wrong.

All these torments and more arise both from the outer impossibilities and the inner ones. On the outside, we are faced with taboos and obstacles that make it impossible to live our passion openly and freely. Our lover may be married and unavailable, or in another city and country, or bound by responsibilities that limit his or her time and availability. More than likely, he or she is also part of a taboo group that renders our love not only difficult, but inappropriate and unacceptable. We alternate between the delight and pride of finding someone "of our own sort" at last and the shame of having chosen someone so wrong. Our choice of lover puts us into conflict with our milieu, and we feel badly for imposing our "madness" on those close to us.

Sometimes, even worse, our choice of lover puts us into conflict with our own deepest values, the milieu inside ourselves where there are also rules and standards we want to abide by. For these impossible situations do not usually choose lawless renegades as their victims. On the contrary, they often strike those with the highest standards. That is exactly their point, and our pain. More often than not, these are people who have set up their lives around a very specific inner image of what is right and what is wrong and who have tried very hard to conform to their own ideals.

They are nearly always individuals of considerable complexity who have not known how to espouse that complexity and so have tried to simplify it into a more acceptable image of apparent unity. Often, consciously or unconsciously, they have had to repress other parts of their personality in order to create this image of rightness and to fit in with the milieu they have chosen to join and function in. The pure schoolteacher, the virtuous lawyer, the caring therapist, the reformer politician, the upright journalist. These are some of the masks or personas our lovers have taken on in order to fit in.

Just because they are masks does not mean they are false, however. On the contrary, these personas do reflect a genuine ego ideal and genuine desire to live out this ideal. They are not just there for show. The problem is simply that they do not express the whole person. They hide parts of the personality not only from the world, but from the wearer of the mask. It is these other parts that come to claim their due in the eruption of impossible love, and they make us feel at war with ourselves. The cement we thought we had built our psychic houses on turns into sand as our dearest values dissolve in the name of passion.

For the aim of impossible love is unerring. It always goes straight to the heart of our most cherished images and values. The things we had said we would never do are exactly the ones we end up doing. When we say, "I could forgive myself or another for anything but . . . ," it is the crime following the "but" that we will probably commit—i.e., have a love affair with a married person, with a patient, with someone of the wrong sex, or someone twenty years our junior, and at the same time betray someone or something we vowed we would always be loyal to: our spouse, our children, our colleagues, our professional duties. To make matters worse, we expand on the crimes we actually commit by imagining ones we had never even considered before; not only would they have been unthinkable, they did not even exist in our psychic storehouses. Then we have the upright journalist threatening to publish slanderous articles full of lies to ruin the reputation of the well-known husband of his lover; the caring therapist having fantasies about locking up her patient/lover in a room where no ethics code could ever penetrate; the pure schoolteacher thinking of becoming a whore as she sneaks around from one sordid hotel room to another; the virtuous lawyer beginning to wonder how to use his knowledge to concoct a dirty divorce, etc. Hate, revenge, and pettiness take their place in our hearts next to love and all its goodness. We realize with a start that we could indeed kill.

This loss of innocence about our own personalities and the standards we thought were water-tight comes eventually to strike us in the most painful place of all—the object of our passion. Not only have we lost our sense of rightful belonging to our own group, and then the sense of integrity we had worked to attain, but also we are soon forced to admit that our partner in passion is, like us, as much devil as god. To paraphrase the famous story made into a film by Singer, we are Enemies, and it is a Love Story. The cliché of "I can't live with you and can't live without you" goes through our head, but it is no longer a cliché. The very person for whom we have risked everything—and through whom we have lost our innocence about ourselves—turns out to be as much enemy as accomplice in this very passion.

Again and again, our lover acts impossibly, making it hard to know whether we can go on or must stop. We wonder if we are kidding ourselves into believing in a "Grand Passion," when it may in fact just be a "Grand Hoax." Rendezvous are missed or cancelled, promises are not kept, messages are contradictory, hopes soar only to be dashed. Like Heloïse, we begin to ask ourselves if we have been the plaything of a person incapable of loving. We, of course, like Heloïse, feel totally capable of loving, and loving all, including the Other's incapacity for loving. If only she/he would see the light and just let it happen. We feel frustrated, furious at our lover because it seems so simple. If only we followed the feelings together, somehow it could all work out, we are sure.

That would be true if the impossibilities were only outer ones, as in the case of my therapist friend and her patient who became lover and then husband. For them, the inner unity was such that it conquered and transformed the outer obstacles. Their relationship could be called unorthodox, but not impossible. On the other hand, when the impossibility defines the passion from within our psyches as well, then we enter into the same situation we saw with Abelard and

Heloïse—two separate truths hiding behind one love. Even in the darkest moments of passion, it is hard to acknowledge that the conflicts we are living already speak more about an individual voyage than a shared adventure. The unconscious energies that have brought us together will also pull us apart, continually, again and again, till we feel literally split apart.

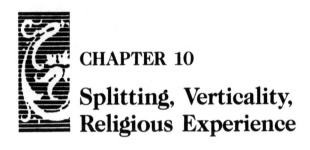

CHAPTER 10

Splitting, Verticality, Religious Experience

Upside Down

The splitting and disunity are intrinsic to impossible love. They are there in the original inequality of the social positions of the lovers and the imbalance of power that makes these loves so wrong in conventional eyes. They are there in the removal of each lover from his or her own milieu and every time "real life" in this milieu calls one or the other back again. Ultimately, this constant splitting moves the love into an otherworldly level in which passion will follow its course—up and down, the highest and the lowest, the worst and the best.

All these contrasts point not to equality and harmony and stasis, but to verticality and dissonance. Unlike possible love where there is some degree of horizontality on earth to share and relate in, impossible love puts us on a vertical axis of uncontrollable ups and downs. Passion may have brought us together, but on its pole we will keep passing each other on the way, struggling in vain to linger together a while, in the same place at the same time.

Psychologically, we identify this verticality and asymmetry when we begin to feel caught in a power struggle with the very person we want most to "just love." Putting a more clinical label on it, we wonder if we aren't acting out a sado-masochistic relationship where pain and power seem to have much more room than caring and mutuality. What is more, the original inequality starts turning upside down and around and around as each person assigns absolute power to the other, and absolute vulnerability to him or herself. The apparently weaker person has as much, if not more, power to upset the apparently stronger one as vice versa, for in passion there is no such thing as only weak or only strong. There is only mutual influence and mutual blindness about this influence. As we shall see in the coming chapters, these power struggles and misunderstandings are indispensable to the tension of passion and its message in our individual lives.

Collision of the Sacred and Profane

If we stay for the moment, however, on an archetypal level and follow our vertical axis up and down, we begin to perceive that it is not for nothing that we have been referring to heaven and hell, for we indeed entered into religion when we said yes to passion. The language we use, the feelings we express, the greatness of it all belong, not to mortal love, but to divine adoration. Like Heloïse, who put Abelard at the center of her own religion and never recanted the heresy—even at the end of her life—in passion we all become believers and put our lover on the altar of our newly found temple.

We revel in serving the object of our love, in devoting time we have, and time we don't have, to glorifying his or her Name. We find ourselves talking and thinking in religious terms, exalted by our own conversion, and challenged by the trials our faith is put to. Even our hell finds its place, adding to our luster as we burn for the cause. For the first time in our lives, we may understand the mystic's desire for ecstatic surrender to the godhead.

We are caught here in the contradiction or paradox of impossible love in which *desire emerges simultaneously in its most profane and most sacred form.* On the one hand, we must have this person, this particular, unique human person, to ourselves in all his or her foibles and charming eccentricities. On the other, we must have access to the divine that this person has put us in contact with, and though we know in our heads the divine and the person are not the same, in our hearts we don't believe this for a minute. Meanwhile, since our lover has also put us on a pedestal and turned us into the god or goddess of his or her new religion, we are totally at cross purposes, "worshipping at a different altar,"[1] I with my image of You, and you with your image of Me.

All this takes place unconsciously, of course. We may know what we are doing, but we don't really understand where we are doing it from and what gods are driving us. We are still in a state of innocence about the forces we naively consented to follow, and so like good acolytes we go on acting out our religion without understanding or questioning its nature. At some moments, we compete as to who can prostrate him or herself the most, and we push each other relentlessly back on the pedestal of absolute power in order to maintain our new servitude and discipleship. These are the moments we look back on later and call "masochistic."

At other moments, we struggle to be adored as is our due, and we do everything to exercise our power and seduction in order to win over the Other as "subject." In these moments, though we rarely admit or even see it, we often act quite sadistically, demanding that our lovers show recognition of the inner greatness and specialness we have always known was there, but rarely dared to express or believe in. At still other moments, we suddenly tire of this game and try to take the other as well as ourselves off all pedestals by attacking or fleeing. These are the moments when our reality ego takes over temporarily and decides it's all ridiculous and that there are better things to do with one's life. However, since the passion does not take place in this everyday reality, our defiance will not usually have much effect. The fact is that both lovers have become indispensable divinities for each other, and yet each remains a fallible human being.

Somehow, impossible love has accomplished the dubious miracle of making a person, actually two people, into a unique combination of human and divine at the same time. We have become demi-gods and demi-devils for each other, and as such there is no going back. Or forward. There is just going up and then down again. In adoration or in blasphemy, in prostration or omnipotence, but rarely in peace, hand in hand.

At this stage, we are like Abelard and Heloïse who could no longer hear each other or take in the human reality of the other in the years after their mutual passion. We are as if enchanted, enrapt by our own experience and vision of love. The more the love continues to be impossible, the more our vision grows about it, and the more this, our unconscious separate truth, grows, the more our actual lover seems to act contrary to our vision and thus to betray our love. He or she may come to be the worst enemy of the very religion he or she "founded" in our hearts, and like Jesus we feel betrayed from within. We do not yet realize that we "need" this betrayal, as Jesus "needed" Judas, in order to transform our vision into something new. On the contrary, like the disciples in the garden of Gethsemane, we just see the betrayal as leading to death.

Sweet Death

In fact, the fantasy and image of death is ever present in impossible love. Very early on, the lovers might find themselves uttering the surprising words "I'd like to die with him/her," and when they reflect on the meaning of their words, they realize they express a desire for ultimate, final consummation. The feeling of joy and oneness is so great and such an accomplishment in the face of so many obstacles that there seems nowhere else to go. Better to end it all now, together, go out in a blaze of absolute immolation before life conspires to ruin the perfection.

The darker, more painful fantasy of death, however, only enters in later, when hope is at a nadir and all seems lost. Such was the case with an analysand, a doctor in a penal institution who had lived a disastrous impossible love with a woman prisoner. He came into my office and announced that, if I could not help him regain a reason to live within a month, he would kill himself. As a doctor, he had the knowledge and material to do this easily. He and the woman had lived a powerful passion for several months. He had illegally arranged special passes for her in order for them to see each other. One day, however, she was not at their rendezvous. She had used her freedom to escape, and the whole story broke. His reputation had been smeared all over the tabloids; his lover had left him to deal with the mess alone. There seemed, indeed, ample reason to think of ending it all.

With time, however, he began to accept that *something needed to die* and that this was already nearly accomplished. His desire to kill himself was like a last stand of ego pride before coming to the painfully disturbing realization that no one had betrayed him but himself. His lover, his shame, the press were simply accomplices to his own inner Judas; and he needed to forgive and make room for this betrayer if he were to emerge, not intact, but transformed through his adventure.

He was a man who had lived only through appearance, prestige, status, and power. The ideals of his youth had quickly given way to cynicism, an obsession with money, and belonging to the right class of people. Falling in love with a criminal was the worst thing that could happen to his pride and vanity, but it made him "die" to certain false values and illusions about himself and, most of all, meet his own "criminal," i.e., not-right and not-conformist, self.

At first, however, his main desire coming into therapy was to go back to the way it had been before, to regain his standing, his sense of himself as an irreproachable professional. Such a "restoration of the persona" was not possible, however. If it had been, then the passion would have just been dalliance, a trivial footnote in a superficial life, and a reprehensible legal mistake. Like the politician caught with a prostitute, he could have repented and vowed never to sin again. He would have paid his dues to society and eventually been restored to good standing, all forgiven and forgotten.

But there was love, not "just sex." This became clear when he could relate back to the feelings he had had with this woman and realized he would do it all again. Yes, he regretted the consequences, but not the love. Since there really was this love, it became vital for him to come to terms with the effects it had on his inner life as well as his outer, to swallow the shame and to use the mutilation not as a moral lesson, but as a wound that could lead him into the depths of his being.

The death of his hard-won persona and social identity was terribly painful, as it was for Abelard, as it is for anyone. Losing his heart to a prisoner destroyed all his illusions about his own invincibility and moral superiority, but also exposed the values he had taken on in his adult life. The ostracization from his peers forced him to look for the first time into his individual beliefs and question what he wanted from his life. His lover was gone, but she had re-awakened a vivifying energy from his forgotten idealistic youth, and gradually he began to want to redirect his life in accordance with some of these ideals translated into adult terms.

The degree to which changes took place was visible in a gesture he made that carried more significance than it would seem. One day he came into my office looking a little different than usual. I didn't know why exactly, and when he asked, a bit shyly, if I found anything different in his appearance, he pointed to his head at the same time. Then I realized that for the first time he was not wearing a toupée. He was in fact totally bald, and he said that he had decided to "show" himself exactly that way, as he really was, with no artificial cover between him and his own truth. On one level he had truly died, but not in the way he had imagined or threatened. He had died to his own fears and artifices, and through an impossible love with a criminal he began to know what it could be like to live as a free man.

Not all impossible love stories are so dramatic, but in nearly all a kind of death occurs. Ultimately, there may be re-birth as well, if the experience of the darkness leads to new insight. The gods may offer initiation, but every lover has to find the personal message hidden in the mystery. In order for the unconscious energies that were let loose in passion to become "humanized," personal and psychological material needs to be joined to the collective and archetypal. Each individual must ask his or her own questions around the meaning of the taboos, the extremes, the light and the darkness in the particular impossible love. In the following section, we shall look into these very human factors.

PART IV

Long-Forgotten Dramas:
Impossible Love and Personal Psychology

CHAPTER 11

The Universal Wounds of Childhood

Fear and Confusion in Impossible Love

Impressive as its extremes may be, the experience of impossible love does not just provoke mystic flights into the heights and the depths. From the everyday vantage point of the lovers, what it brings above all is confusion and fear. Everything is mixed-up—feelings, roles, and ego certainties. What is more, since we have stepped out of our own safe boundaries in order to love, we inevitably fall into the unknown, and this is frightening. Though all love includes some fear—of loss, of abandonment, of engulfment—in impossible love we must add those which arise from being with the "wrong person."

What is wrong may actually be illegal, as in the case of patients and therapists in California where it is a felony for the therapist to have a sexual relation-ship with a patient at any time in his or her life. The wrong combination of lovers may also consist of stu-dent/teacher, client/lawyer, parishioner/priest, or any less official, but nevertheless unequal and frowned-upon form of love, such as rich/poor, married/single, young/old, sophisticated/naive. In all these situations, when love enters, it brings not just hope, but corrosive fear.

Professionals panic at the fear of being accused of abusing their more innocent clients; clients fear entering into the impressive worlds of their lovers or wonder if they are really loved, or just victims. The rich older person fears being seen as a corrupter of minors, while the younger, poorer partner fears being seen as a mercenary exploiter. The more established, sophisticated individual fears the shame of being associated with someone not quite on his or her level, and the more marginal or naive one fears being seen as too socially inept for such a personage. Fears about what people will think, fears about the consequences of such a love, fears about how it may or may not work out.

In many ways, the fears are founded. Seeing the inequality and difficulties of the relationship, some people will, and do, think exactly what you fear they will. The basic inequalities will also cause some impossible dilemmas in the relationship itself, as we have seen in preceding chapters.

But, even worse than all these fears about objective problems is the confusion created in the psyche of the individual lovers. Suddenly nothing is what it seemed. Conventional roles and expectations are turned upside down as we follow the lure of passion through to the other side of the looking glass. Senses become ethereal, God becomes sex, child turns into parent, and vice versa. Animus and anima take over where men and women leave off. He becomes a prin-

LONG-FORGOTTEN DRAMAS

cess in a tower besieged; she turns into a prince, braving heights and arrows to rescue him. Somehow the opposites have all met and exploded at once. As one half of an impossible couple, we leave the familiar "me" and enter into an underworld where we partake of a new and confusing multiplicity of being. We may meet our souls there, but we lose our usual ego boundaries and identity.

How on earth could things get so mixed up? How could a patient have such power over a doctor, or a youngster over a seasoned adult? And even more than how, why? What is it in us that wants to embrace that Other so much that we will transgress the borders of our own safe reality in order to love wrongly?

Childhood Gone Wrong

In analyzing some of the psychological factors that contribute to a person's involvement in impossible love, we need to go back to the personal past. We have seen that the energy of passion puts us on a vertical otherworldly axis, but to understand the passion's individual message we need to change to a horizontal one. Impossible love does not just link heaven and hell. If we are willing, it can also lead us back to our own beginnings, and from there forward into a more original future, one that is not just determined by what happened way back then.

The taboos, the inequalities, the clash of opposites, the misunderstandings, the hopes, and disappointments have already taken place in our lives long before we meet the Great Love. As children, we met them early on and, in the meeting, also learned about impossible love.

There is no single cause to these early disappointments. There is no particular kind of family that makes them inevitable. To some extent, all children are wounded because no parents can be perfect. From a child's point of view, the first experience of life is not of entering into a family in the social sense of the word, but of arrival into a Universe run by gods that reign supreme. Mother and Father are the deities who provide everything from food, to comfort, to life itself. Ideally, they are loving, benevolent gods who want only the best for their offspring. But most parents are not equipped to be gods, and some are barely equipped to be parents. No one teaches a parent how to parent, and even in the best of cases, mistakes will be made that will have a lasting effect on the children.

Often, in spite of the mistakes, the environment is adequate, or "good enough," as the well-known child psychologist Winnicott would say, to provide basic emotional and material welfare. But often it is not. For all sorts of reasons—ignorance, hardship, immaturity, illness, alcoholism, and so forth—many parents just cannot give what the children need. As Barbara Sullivan writes in her thoughtful book *Therapy Grounded in the Feminine Principle*, "The universal human wound is the one that comes from the *failure of the environment to adequately meet the needs of the individual*."[1] This wound is all the more universal in that each child has such unique psychological needs above and beyond the basic material ones that already demand so much from parents. Few parents have the time or the wisdom to be exactly in tune all the time to what each of their children needs at each of their stages in growth.

Intellectually, we all know this. As adults, we real-ize that our parents were human beings who did their best, or didn't, but did give us life and sent us on our way. But the child within does not necessarily agree with this reasonable point of view. The child in all of us is often still longing for the Perfect Family That Wasn't.

Since most of us grew up in families that were very un-ideal, we do not imagine that the right kind of family would simply be adequate, or good enough. On the contrary, in order to compensate for all the wounds and lacks we experienced as children, we tend to create an inner model of the ideal family that con-tinues to influence us long after we have left home.

One very thorough description of such a perfect family has emerged over the years from seminars I have given around the Mother Archetype and aspects of the Feminine and Masculine. As an exercise, to draw out some of our unconscious ideals, I ask the par-ticipants to brainstorm on their idea of the perfect parents. As they speak, I transcribe what they say on the blackboard until we have a list that fills up both sides and runs off the edges. The more I write, the more we all laugh, because as the list grows, it be-comes somehow hilarious to see the sheer abundance of our childlike ideals. On a more serious note, we begin to realize that no matter how grown up we are, we still carry these ideals inside, and they have quite an influence on how we act in everyday life. With the help of television, psychology books, and our own imaginations, we come to conceive of a mythical perfect family that looks something like the following.

The Perfect Family Everyone Should Have Had

In this modern version of the Perfect Family, the mother is confident of her femininity and yet sure of herself in the workplace. She feels no conflict between children, husband, work, and her own needs. She is gentle and loving and protective with the children when they are babies. She empathetically responds to their cries and knows instinctively what each sound or gesture means in this early stage of total dependency. Hunger, loneliness, fatigue, wet diapers, sickness are all clearly decoded and understood by this in-tune mother. As the babies grow into youngsters and grow away from the initial, symbiotic relationship with her, she encourages the separation, yet is present and comforting when they need to return to be dependent on her once again.

This mother loves all her children equally. She promotes their different interests and understands that each has a particular way of expressing him or herself. She never envies them their youth or talent because she has always engaged her own creativity. What is more, she understands that, at a certain age, they will want to spend more time with their father than with her. She feels a pang of regret for the years they depended more on her, but she can honestly admit this. Such passing jealousy, therefore, will cause no trouble because she has owned it, and above all because she recognizes that it is normal for the children to idealize their father as they grow toward adulthood. She knows it is indispensable to their psychological health to have a model for the masculine pole of affirmation and achievement, so that their own inner hero or heroine gets constellated and allows them to go forth, full of confidence, into the world outside the safety of the home.

In her role of wife, this ideal woman is strong and yet supportive, understanding and yet her own person. She never nags or complains about her husband to the children. She never abdicates the work of disciplining to him either, for she knows it is important that the children realize that men and women can both be firm and loving. She never loses her own sense of identity in the demanding daily round of mother, spouse, and worker. She remains sexually attractive and vital, well-dressed and physically fit despite her busy schedule. She also continues to be a stimulating partner for her husband, interested in the world outside, even as she tends to the emotional temperature and well-being of the family.

As for the father in this hypothetical family, he is serene and sure of himself as man and parent. He has shared in the process of pregnancy and birth, and he shares just as much afterwards in the children's upbringing. He may feel some jealousy about the mother/child dyad in the earliest time of the children's lives, but most of all he is bursting with pride to be a father, whether of a boy or a girl. He understands his wife's fatigue in the months after birth and is present to relieve her and provide both her and the infant with a sense of security and love.

As the children grow, he gives special attention to each and encourages them to take risks, to learn new things, to be curious and unafraid in the world. He does not push the boys too hard but challenges them to new tasks, giving them confidence in their young masculinity. With the girls, he also encourages risk-taking so that they will not be dependent on men in later life. At the same time, he appreciates their youthful femininity and makes them feel glad to be born women.

Although he does not refuse to make his authority felt when necessary, he admits when he is wrong and knows how to relate emotionally with his children. He has great hopes for their futures, but puts no pressure on any child to live out his own unfulfilled dreams because he, like his wife, is satisfied in his marriage and work.

As husband, this ideal man is attentive, caring, and demonstrative. He expresses his needs clearly in the marriage and knows his wife will do the same. Together, they form a bonded couple, affectionate and as in love at forty as they were at twenty. They have crises in their marriage like any couple, but they are mature enough to work out the differences together and never involve the children in those tensions.

For all this perfection, these parents are not squares. They know how to let their hair down and have fun, just as they know when to be disciplined and serious.

For the children, the benefits of growing up in such a household would theoretically be manifold. Because of their mother's capacity for being a good enough caretaker early on, who responded empathetically to their infant needs, none of them will grow up out of tune with their own bodies. They will not have eating disorders or other addictions. They will naturally be drawn to healthy choices for their physical well-being.

Because their father encouraged them and shared his knowledge with them, they will go confidently into the world as young adults and not have problems of self-esteem or an "imposter" complex. They will be lucid about their own limits and potential and undertake exactly what suits them professionally. The girls will feel naturally attractive to men without needing to resort to excessive seduction. The boys will be respectful of women while feeling unashamed of their own assertive energy.

More than just the mother and father, however, it is the couple as a pair which will have a positive effect on the children's lives. Having had as a model a man and woman who loved and respected each other, they will feel assured in their relationships with the other sex. They will neither expect nor attract any neurotic acting out between men and women. Fear of commitment, dependency problems, difficulty in communications, cruelty, or "loving too much" will not be part of the picture in their personal lives. Having grown up with two mature, creative adults, they will quickly recognize maturity and creativity in others and be unlikely to love the "wrong" kind of individual. Since their parents did not indulge in splitting and competition at home, the children will not be tempted to favor or mistrust either sex. They will not be unduly competitive with their siblings, and this cooperative attitude will carry on with their peers in later life. Envy and jealousy will not have a chance to take root in their psychology.

This is all the more true in that their ideal parents believed in appreciating the differences among all people and did not indulge in scapegoating when someone was unlike themselves. They did not feel they had to submit or adapt to each other in order to be loved, and they did not demand that of their children. Being sensitive and intelligent human beings, they were able to discern the particular gift of each child and put no taboos on creativity or expression, no matter how eccentric or different from their own taste.

Yet, there were rules to be followed, and clear limits were established as far as community living was concerned. These children were socialized appropriately and never felt subsequently ill at ease about how to behave in public. Rules did not mean repression, however. Sexuality was natural, love was flowing and affectionate. Even negative feelings had their place as part of normal life, and no one was ever judged for expressing anger or other unsociable emotions. In fact, each child was encouraged to keep a diary from very early on as a way of cultivating their inner life. Dreams, feelings, fantasy were regularly discussed and applauded around the dinner table.

As a result of this very healthy upbringing, the children would enter into adult life with few psychological problems. They would probably not fall in love impossibly. They would not have to transgress taboos in order to discover their true selves. They would not be torn between the conflicting desires of their grownup and child selves. They would reach adulthood with equal interest in outer accomplishment and the inner life. Having successfully passed through the different childhood phases of dependency and revolt, idealization and rejection, they would likely enter into healthy marriages and satisfying professional lives and go on to raise gifted children of their own.

The Reality

In reality, we all know that no one grows up like this. In fact, it would probably be extremely stressful to have such perfect parents. Yet, harmless and funny as these ideals seem, the fairy-tale image they project may tyrannize us for years as we unconsciously strive to make up for the failure of our parents. Most of the excessively positive traits we ascribe to the ideal parents come right out of our own emotional deprivation. *What my mother or father was not, I will be. What they did not do, I will do.* A woman may spend a good part of her adult life denying her own needs for dependency and vulnerability because she saw her own mother collapse under the weight of her helplessness. Another one may get over-involved in her children's lives because her own mother was disinterested or too overwhelmed by other cares to be available. A man may deny his own sexuality in order not to be macho like his father or take on too much responsibility and become a workaholic to avoid repeating the failure of an under-employed father.

Just as we were not loved unconditionally as children and were not seen for what we really were, in later life we have trouble releasing ourselves from the rigid inner ideals we have evolved in order to offset the effects of our—this less-than-ideal—former environment. The high standards we set for ourselves may aim to make us better than our parents, and irreproachable in the eyes of the world, but they do not leave much room for love and creativity. To identify more precisely what the failures of love were in our childhood, we need only look more closely at the details of the Perfect Family we just described. When we see through its paradisical colors, we can easily guess at the negative reality it is compensating for.

Though emotional lacks and failures of love vary in quality and kind from family to family and child to child, there are certain constants in most situations where the environment is not good enough. In these cases, mother and father do not love well and do not present a unified image of male and female energies working in tandem. The gods that rule over the child's universe are often at war, or estranged, and the child does not grow up with an inner sense of balance between Yang and Yin, masculine and feminine. Power and love, affirmation and receptivity, become vying forces rather than complementary ones.

Just as myths and fairy tales tell us, when the king and the queen are separated or in conflict, all the kingdom suffers and the subjects, i.e., the children in this case, necessarily feel the effects of such discord. The child does not yet know that there are other "kingdoms," other families where things are different. He or she has no choice but to adapt to the circumstances created by his or her particular parents and quickly learns what to avoid and what to show in order not to be expelled from the only known world.

Unlike our mythical perfect family, in this troubled setting, taboos and inequalities are established around modes of expression and ways of being. Love may be elusive and unpredictable, too much or too little at a time. When parents are chronically dissatisfied with each other and with their lives, their ability to love is naturally diminished. As human beings with unfulfilled needs, they cannot help but relate to their children as much, if not more, out of their own needs, as out of any needs the children might have. Since children need love as much as food to grow, they will do what is necessary to follow the rules, be good and worthy of love, even if it means sacrificing parts of their own personalities.

The False Self and
Other Defenses to Survive

Alice Miller, in her book *The Drama of the Gifted Child*, gives us a pointed description of the main consequences of such sacrifices. She points out that, when children must over-adapt to their parents' needs, they lose touch with their own deepest feelings, especially the "negative" ones such as anger, jealousy, envy, anxiety, despair, or fear.[2] Such feelings are not allowed or welcomed by the parents who need their children to admire and support them and not make waves. Like the subjects of capricious royalty, these children grow up to be either "yes men" or dissidents. In either case, their childhood was devoted more to reacting to parental rules and moods than to developing their own complex personalities.

They may arrive in adulthood with a psychological veneer that Miller and other specialists call the False Self. The Self that makes us do what we think is expected of us is compliant and good, accommodating and adapted. It is what I have called, in another context, the Schoolgirl Complex, a complex that women particularly suffer from when they spend their lives working to get good grades from all the projected authorities "out there"—men, institutions, etc. But this False Self may also take the form of an inner hero or heroine that pushes the person to remarkable feats of performance and achievement that comply with outer values, but do not fulfill inner needs.

In fact, whatever the form of the False Self that

emerges from having to cope with a dysfunctional family situation, *the greatest tragedy is always the loss of genuine inner life.* Whether we get caught in trying to be what our parents demanded or, just as bad, by our own rigid inner ideal of being what the parents were not, we are unable to live the foolishness, risk-taking, openness, and vulnerability that make for a sense of creativity and fulfillment in life. Sullivan makes this observation when she notes that "In ordinary outpatient practice, the universal problem is the patient's loss of his inner reality."[3] Note again her use of the word "universal." Just as the wounds of most patients in therapy are universal, so is this loss of inner reality. It is not just an aberration that happens to a few unfortunate individuals who grew up with especially evil parents. *It is a very widespread problem in a culture that does not value the inner life in general and does little or nothing to help parents foster their own or that of their children.*

The individuals who do enter therapy are often the ones who are the most sensitive to this loss. If therapists see so many patients in their thirties, forties, and fifties, it is because by then the adapting mechanisms of childhood are beginning to falter. The defenses that were created to survive and establish a social identity are not adequate to bring deeper kinds of satisfaction, but it often takes a crisis to precipitate a questioning of these defensive strategies. An impossible love, a divorce, a major loss, an illness are some of the ways life forces us to stop and ask the questions we need to ask if we are to change directions and leave the world of childhood values. It is too late to go back and undo the original wounds of love and trust, but not too late to understand how they drove us to build a fortress that both protected us from harm and kept us from living. We may protest about the crises that drive us into therapy or upset our well-laid plans, but our protest is too late, for, as Aldo Carotenuto, author of *Eros and Pathos*, points out,

> The loss we fear ... has already occurred. We no longer have a father and mother to protect us, and if we nourish such hope it is but an illusion—so fervent an illusion that it even succeeds in creating in the outer world parental images that perpetuate the existence of our real mother and father. *When one understands that one has already lost all, then one begins to take up the cudgel with oneself.*[4]

I would just add to his words "the existence of our real mother and father" the words *"our parents as we wished they had been,"* for when real parents are truly nourishing and protective, their children do not grow up with a need to entertain illusions of finding perfect, parental benevolence in the world of outer authorities and other people. They do not need to exhaust themselves in the compulsive search for the perfect love. This search, as we have seen, is the result of failure, a failure that is often too painful for a child to cope with other than by adapting and surviving. Only later on can the individual find the strength to confront the childhood losses. Impossible love is one of the ways life forces us to come to terms with these losses and "to take up the cudgel with ourselves."

The Timing: Inner Readiness and Love

Paradoxically, for those individuals whose individuation process passes by way of the experience of an impossible love, when it does arrive it is often a sign that the psyche is strong enough to face the pain of the past. People do not fall into passionate love as long as their survival mechanisms are still intact and necessary. They may have affairs, and even be married, and go along contentedly for years, but never feel the sting of passion. We do not lose our hearts and our self-control on command.

In a book on love's "shock" effect, the Italian author Alberoni states in fact that "There is no relationship between the desire to be in love and the actual act of falling in love."[5] He goes on to describe how a person may long for love, look for love, complain constantly that he or she is missing love, and yet not meet that special person who provokes the "fall." Falling in love has nothing to do with willpower and everything to do with readiness, especially inner readiness. We are open to passion when we are open to change.

Whether we realize it or not, something in us is dissatisfied with our existence, so dissatisfied that we are available to love's revolutionary impact.[6] Falling in love always signals a need to end a certain status quo and to begin to create a new world. When the love is from all objective points of view an impossible one besides, then the revolution will be an inner event. *The arrival of impossible love always announces a need for psychological change and questioning of the past.*

In the story of Abelard and Heloïse, we saw some of the major changes their unliveable love brought to their lives. Because we know too little of their childhoods, however, it is difficult to make pertinent psychological connections between the love they shared and the early events that may have contributed to their mutual attraction. Rather than venture into psycho-biography, let us look at the story of a modern woman who in a way combines aspects of both Abelard and Heloïse in her meeting with impossible love.

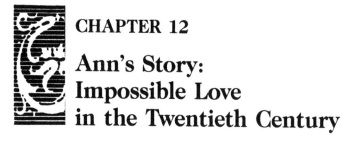

CHAPTER 12

Ann's Story: Impossible Love in the Twentieth Century

I first met Ann when she entered into analysis look-ing for answers to her problem of impossible love. Pro-fessionally, she was almost as successful in her time and place as Abelard was in his. Personally, however, she felt as helpless to live out her love life as Heloïse. The first time I saw her, it was hard to believe she could be a victim of anything or anyone. She was forty-ish, extremely attractive in a classic Ralph Lauren manner, very articulate, and obviously intelligent. Everything about and on her matched—her clothes, her hairdo, her make-up were all "right." Only the ex-pression of tension and fear on her face gave away the inner drama that had driven her to pick up the phone and ask for an appointment. She could no longer go it alone, she said. She was in love, head over heels; and terrified of what was happening. Over the months that followed, she related her story of great outer success and equally great difficulty and despair in her love life—difficulties that seemed to get worse, not better, with time.

Ann taught sociology at a local university. She was on a tenure track; she was respected in her field and loved the work of teaching and research. In many ways, she was a self-made woman, having paid her way through college by modeling and other jobs. She had left her family at nineteen and never looked back.

The personal life of this independent woman was mostly composed of several friendships of long standing. As for her love life, until she was about thirty-five, there was "no problem," she said. She had been married briefly in her early twenties to a charming drifter who worked odd jobs. He was jealous and unpredictable, and after he had beaten her up several times in the course of six months, Ann proceeded to divorce him. Since that time she had vowed never to lose her heart again.

What Ann understood about this disastrous liaison was that it was a way of rebelling against her conventional background to marry a man from a a working class background and one who was openly violent as well. She had never looked any deeper into her own psychology to ask why she found herself with such an individual. At the time, she had enough on her plate to get out of the marriage and get her life back on track. Later, she would even laugh about the episode as an example of her "pre-feminist" naïveté.

For several years she continued to put all her energy into her career and did not meet any man who touched her heart. Like many of her women friends, she lamented that there were no interesting men anyway, but basically, as she admitted later, she simply was not available to love in these years. She did, however, have several affairs and broke some hearts on the way, for many men fell in love with her. This both flattered and exasperated her. It also left her feeling lonely, for as she said, "At least the men who loved me had their pain to keep them company. I had nothing but feelings of guilt." She was not yet aware of her power as a woman and her need to hurt men by seducing and rejecting them. She could not know then that she was repeating with her suitors what had been done to her as a child, holding out the promise of love and then pulling it back with an innocent air of "Who, me?"

The First Impossible Love: The Right Heart and the Wrong Taste

This kind of consciousness only came when, at last, she did fall in love, wrongly, impossibly, and painfully. She fell at thirty-five, she fell at thirty-seven, and she had fallen again at forty when I met her. After all the years of insulated protection from her feelings, suddenly she was ready for the change that passion ushers in, but like most of us, Ann resisted its message as long as she could.

The first love affair was with Paul, a salesman she met on a plane when she was en route to an academic conference. He was everything the men she usually frequented were not. He was warm, funny, demonstrative, and uninhibited about showing affection in public. For the first time in years, Ann felt like a woman and not just a collegial talking head. Her femininity and sexuality, so long locked-up, blossomed with her salesman lover. Unfortunately, her critical mind was never far behind. "He" pointed out to Ann that Paul made serious grammar mistakes when he spoke, wore polyester shirts in the summer, and thought paté was a poor substitute for meatloaf.

Much to Ann's surprise, when her critical mind was not working, she liked to be included in the company of Paul's friends and family. She liked their straightforwardness and lack of pretension and felt seen for herself and not just her diplomas. Yet, the relationship did not work out. Although she liked going into his world, Ann could not bring herself to introduce this person into *her* milieu. His taste, his language, his manners were too wrong. Ann was ashamed of her uncouth lover. She tried to rationalize, tried to tell herself not to be such a snob, that he could learn if she gave him a chance, that love had nothing to do with taste. But such fair-minded arguments were to no avail. The shame won out, and Ann ended the relationship, full of sadness and regret but unable to bear the tension between her private feelings and her public persona. Her friends and colleagues never even had a chance to express the judgments she feared. She did it for them, as her own inner taboos triumphed.

These taboos were ones she had interjected from the tensions between her parents. Her father had rejected and devalued the working-class background of his wife. Ann and her siblings had had little contact with the maternal line of the family, but what she remembered was a feeling of warmth and unpretentiousness. It was not for nothing she had felt "surprisingly at ease" with Paul's family. It was as if, by loving him, she was allowing herself to re-establish a connection with her maternal heritage. Such a literal way to do this, however, was unworkable. She could not, at thirty-five, repair the injustices her father had dealt her mother when Ann was a child. Besides, at this point in her emotional life, she did not yet recognize that the ambivalence she felt about Paul repeated a family drama already played out. Such recognition would not come until other dramas were enacted in her own life.

The Second Impossible Love:
Good Taste and Inaccessibility

The next time Ann fell in love, it was with great relief. This time, she said to herself, I'm doing it "right." The object of her love was a fellow academic, a man of charm and polish. He and Ann were working together on a research project when they found themselves staying late, having a drink together, and then falling in love. With Robert, Ann felt once again on a level of equality. There were no conflicts of taste or culture, no grammar mistakes to flinch over. Robert was brilliant and enjoyed Ann's intelligence. He was funny and enjoyed Ann's sense of humor. She found herself entertaining him with stories of her hapless salesman lover who thought meatloaf was better than paté. She had quickly forgotten the pain of her love affair with Paul and had already turned it into a dinner table anecdote.

The only thing wrong with her relationship with Robert was that they didn't seem to have much physical contact. Unlike Paul, Robert was discreet and reserved in public, but also, to Ann's dismay, in private. When she finally dared to ask if anything was wrong, he admitted that he was bi-sexual but had not been with a woman since an early marriage many years ago. He went on to explain that he was so attracted to Ann's company, he had hoped that with her he could live a heterosexual relationship once again. Unfortunately, so far he had not felt any physical sensation except affection and warmth.

Ann heard his words but did not see the danger. Whatever Robert's intention, the message she heard behind his words was "If you are a real woman, you will know how to transform me. If you cannot, then you are not a real woman." She understood this as a challenge and, like many women in a similar situation, she could not resist picking up the gauntlet. Since Robert and she got along so well, they both hoped something would move, and Ann hoped she would be the woman who would bring about this change.

For weeks she pondered and fretted over how to be a "real" woman, one seductive and appealing enough to win his heart and especially his body. As she said later, "It was during this time that I began to understand the torment I put my lovers through in the years my heart was still locked-up. It felt like life was taking revenge by putting me on the other side." She consulted psychology books, talked to her friends, tried every conceivable way to please him, but somehow nothing worked. Whether she played hard to get or came on like a vamp, he remained warm, willing, and unable. She felt more and more ashamed of herself and her failure to save her lover. She felt deeply humiliated in the part of herself where she felt the least secure, her feminine sexuality. Like many people in love, however, Ann had her stubborn pride, and the more she suffered, the more she determined to overcome.

In such a situation, it is as if we all have an inner hero or heroine of love that simply cannot give up once it is mobilized. If we cannot be great lovers, at least we can be great martyrs. Sometimes we need to go very far in the pain before we realize we are stuck in a "repetition compulsion," trying to extort love from someone who cannot give it, acting like the children we once were when it was impossible to accept that love was not possible.

Ann was not aware of this repetition; she made no links between her academic lover and her inaccessible father whom she idealized, while at the same time trying in vain to win his affection. Her self-imposed martyrdom with Robert did come to an end, however, as Robert began to feel increasingly guilty about being unable to respond to her rescuing efforts. Rather than lead her on, he tried to gently let her down by honestly saying that he had begun to be interested in a man, and he started to withdraw from the intensity of his and Ann's relationship. Again Ann heard but didn't hear. She could not just turn off the inner heroine and the Pygmalion part of herself that had gotten so involved in the transformation process of Robert. It took a more graphic incident to break the spell and drive her away for good.

One evening, as she was driving home through

a part of town she rarely went to, she stopped at a red light and saw Robert walking down the street with a very young, very good-looking man. She could not help but deduce from the familiarity of their gestures that the two men were lovers. Feeling shocked and betrayed in spite of herself, she drove home, threw up all night, and came down with a flu that kept her in bed for a week.

It took much longer than a week for her psyche to recover, and it would be two years before she fell in love again. During this time she took refuge in her mind the way she had done all her life. With the help of popular psychology books and her women friends, she managed to distance herself from the humiliation by deciding that men were impossible and love a patriarchal trap. Deep down inside she also felt ashamed and inadequate, wondering why she had gotten involved with such inappropriate lovers. Why couldn't she find a "normal" man of her level and interests? What was wrong with her anyway? Blaming men or blaming herself, she was not able to make the more subtle connections between her choice of lovers and her own psychological baggage. She did not see then that both Robert and Paul were more than just mistakes, that they both brought back pieces of her past that she had cut off and thought she was rid of.

Like many individuals who strike out on their own when they are young, Ann was an excellent survivor, but in many ways still a child emotionally. At nineteen she had cut off all connections with her family and gone on to re-invent herself in another world. She had also reconstituted a "family" around herself in the form of friends and colleagues. On the surface this worked well, but psychologically, all the family issues that drove her to leave in the first place remained unresolved. She took the early wounds of love and the dysfunctional family model with her as inner realities, and when her emotional carapace began to break apart at around age thirty-five, she was thrown back into feelings and needs that had been frozen for years, but had never evolved. No wonder she felt so split and humiliated in her love life. She expected by her mid-thirties to finally live the mature, creative love relationship that would be a reward for all her efforts to make a life for herself. Instead, she ended up living relationships that made her behave and feel like "a hysterical victim in a Harlequin romance."

The Third Impossible Love: The Outer Reality Leading to Inner Exploration

The love affair she was engaged in when she came into analysis was the most upsetting of all because she could see no way at all of giving it up or making it possible. It was both more wrong and more right than either of the others. Her lover was a student of hers, ten years younger than she. He was an actor, married with two young children. Ann and he met when she was giving a summer course for adult students, and he attended in order to get credit for a degree he wanted to complete, having dropped out of college to go into theater at age eighteen.

In a way, they each represented what the other

had not done. Peter admired Ann's brilliant mind and professional confidence. Ann was attracted to Peter's marginality and imagination. Both were at a crossroads in their lives, but neither realized it until it was too late. From the moment Peter saw Ann in front of the class, he had said to himself, "I must be with that woman." Less constrained than she by professional concerns, he set about to spend as much time as he could with her.

Ann thought he was charming and enjoyed being the one who introduced him into the world of ideas. For a while they carried on a relationship that seemed innocent enough, protegé and mentor, student and teacher. But just as love sent its arrows into the little schoolroom where Abelard was teaching Heloïse, so it took aim at Ann and Peter as they leaned over a book on sociology. In a moment of shared laughter, they looked at each other and the roles went out the window.

All the taboos were there. Adultery, older woman–younger man, transgression of professional frame. Peter could lose his family. Ann could lose her reputation and livelihood. As is often the case, Ann as the "stronger" member of the couple was much more obsessed with the consequences of their wrongdoing than Peter. It was as if she were obliged to carry the values of the judging super-ego—"Such love affairs are wrong, irresponsible, etc."—while Peter took a stand for the irrational unconscious—"Yes, but we both need what we give each other. It can't be wrong if it is so creative. . . ." Whatever their stand, they both fell into the underworld anyway, a world where ordinary values turned upside down.

Ann felt humiliated by her own professional lapse, terrified someone would find out, unsure of the reality of Peter's love. In a nightly trial in her head, she went back and forth between the inner responsible adult as prosecutor and the inner lover as defendant. The adult brought up all the reasons it could never work—"He is too young, he does not know what he is getting into, it is irresponsible and evil for an older woman to seduce an innocent student." The lover within listened to all these arguments and shrugged her shoulders. When they were together, Ann felt they could re-invent the world. Never had either experienced such an intensity of passion at once physical, emotional, and spiritual.

By the time Ann entered analysis, their relationship had been going on for a year in secret and she was at her wit's end. She pleaded with me from the onset not to tell her "to stop and grow up." She was afraid of any judgments, afraid of her passion— afraid, period.

This was new for Ann. She was an extremely courageous woman who had faced many difficulties on her own, but something in her was crumbling, and it was terrifying for her to feel. I promised I would not tell her to stop the relationship with Peter and asked her to tell me about herself so we could at least begin to find some sense in what she experienced as incomprehensible and frightening. Over the months her tale came out. The tale of her professional trajectory, and the recent disappointments in other love affairs, but also of her childhood.

Inner Discovery: The Wounds of Childhood

Ann had grown up in a family where chaos and conflict were the norm. Her mother was from an Irish working-class background; her father was a Canadian WASP. Her mother was a practical extrovert, her father a dreamy introvert. The two parents had been perhaps attracted to each other as opposites, but they never managed to meet in harmony in the middle. They fought, they denigrated each other, they drank. According to Ann, even in this activity, they expressed their class differences. Her father drank himself into oblivion every evening behind *The Globe and Mail.* Her mother drank herself into nightly scenes that often ended when she woke Ann up in the middle of the night to complain about her husband and passed out on Ann's bed.

Her father worked in the family business, and it was assumed her brother would too. Ann's maternal grandparents lived far away, her mother had little contact with them, and they were considered too lower class to be interesting. Her paternal grandparents made no bones about their dislike of their vulgar daughter-in-law. The universe in which Ann got her first impressions of masculine and feminine values was one that portrayed the masculine as intelligent, refined, and put upon, while the feminine was vulgar, exhibitionist, and never satisfied. Needless to say, Ann decided very early on that she would never be like her mother.

Both parents were extremely unhappy with their lives. Her father had wanted to be an engineer and participate in the conception of innovative building projects in other countries. Instead, he had bowed to his father's demand, returned home after studying business administration, and taken up his role as company heir.

Her mother had wanted to be an actress, but her youthful attempts on stage had proven unsuccessful. When she met Ann's father, she made a decision to give up her tentative career. They married and settled down to life in the suburbs.

In the years afterwards, each parent projected his or her own professional failures on the other, blaming the constraints of marriage for keeping them from a career that neither in fact had had the courage to pursue. They also turned to their children for fulfillment they found neither within themselves or in each other.

Ann's father chose her older sister as his special favorite. She was a beautiful child, with a more pliant personality than Ann's, and she was a natural to play the role of "anima" for a man unable to relate to the woman he had married. He spoiled her, took her on special trips, introduced her to his colleagues at work. He also read her the poetry he wrote in secret that expressed all the feelings he was not able to show in everyday life. As "Daddy's little girl," this sister grew up confident of her power with men but not at all sure of herself as an individual.

She knew how to be seductive and pleasing—her father had rewarded her highly for this. But she did not know how to express her own desires if they conflicted with someone else's. She developed a successful False Self of adaptable femininity that led to an early marriage with the right kind of man, and she moved far away to another province, following her husband's career but also needing to escape the family without seeming to be in rebellion. For both parents she was a "success," the beautiful, dutiful daughter who never challenged their values or authority. Neither parent saw or suspected the price the perfect daughter paid in terms of her own individuality.

Ann did see, but by the time she began to realize the effects of their childhood on both herself and her siblings it was too late to re-connect. As adults, they had all scattered in different directions: her sister into marriage and a home in another province, her brother into the family business, and she into a career on the other side of the continent. Like many children of conflictual family backgrounds, they disidentified with each other, each one determined to do better than their parents, but apart from each other. It was as if their common bond was felt more as a source of remembered pain than a possibility of mutual support.

Just as her sister was her father's favorite, Ann was the child her mother took over as "hers." She was the second born, and since she was not the son eagerly awaited by her father and paternal grandparents, it was tacitly understood that she would be her mother's object of love. Her mother even affirmed her special relationship with Ann by naming her after her own mother. By temperament and looks, Ann was more a rebel and a tomboy than her sister. Photos she showed me of the two together revealed striking differences between them. In a photograph taken for the family Christmas card when Ann was eight and her sister ten, we see the pretty mother bending over her lovely curly-haired eldest as they both smile into the camera. Ann stands on the side, straight-haired, a rather stern and sad look on her face, definitely not the picture of the ideal little girl.

Her tomboy temperament, however, suited her mother who saw her own thwarted adventurousness in Ann. In a strange turnaround of roles, Ann became for her mother what her sister was for her father—a substitute lover who would understand and express all that the parent had not lived. On the one hand, as Ann stated in her pondering on this part of her life, it was not so bad. Her mother encouraged her to be strong and independent, to get good marks in school, to take risks. At the same time, all this encouragement was conditional. In exchange for this parental attention, Ann had to relate in detail all that she did to her mother, who listened avidly while repeating how much Ann resembled her as a child.

Like her sister, Ann got caught in the net of the projection of a parent, but the False Self she developed as a response was different. She did not grow up to be seductive and winning. She grew up to be fearless and invulnerable. She developed what she named her inner "warrior" heroine that was not allowed to feel pain, be tender, or be receptive to her own sensitivity. As she commented, "My mother's need to have an androgynous heroine for a child who would go out and conquer the world in her place certainly gave me an advantage in the world of professional competition, but it did not do much for my femininity."

Ironically, the parent who supported Ann was also the one she most rejected as she was growing up. Her mother's intrusiveness was so great that Ann began to flee outside the house as soon as she could. She visited friends, joined clubs, anything to avoid being pulled in by her mother's neediness and demands. At the same time, and also ironically, she idealized her father more and more, seeing him as the patient, sensitive, intelligent man who was misunderstood by his harridan wife.

Meanwhile, under the influence of drink and disappointment in life, her father was withdrawing more and more from family involvement. As is often the case, such a psychological absence left all sorts of room for Ann to project "misunderstood greatness" into. By the time she left home, she was convinced her mother was the "villain" in the family and her father a great scholar who, but for her mother's nagging, would have been famous and happy. Only after the experiences of her own painful love affairs and after she entered analysis did she begin to revise this vision.

Dreamscape of the Woman Within

More or less consciously, until she was about forty, Ann lived out her warrior values, fighting for success and having little patience with weakness. By then she had not only made a place for herself in the professional area, but also she had quite consciously "overhauled her appearance," as she said. After her first marriage, she had decided to win back her self-respect as a woman by studying how to look the part of the professional she wanted to be. She read women's magazines, carefully controlled her diet, signed up for gym classes, and little by little acquired the impeccable appearance she had when I first saw her. She had succeeded not only in having the career her mother didn't, but in creating a "look" that made her at last as good, if not better, than her sister.

In spite of this perfection, the first dream she spoke of gave an entirely different picture of masculine and feminine values in her psyche. It was a dream that she had had during her relationship with Robert, one that she had never forgotten.

In the dream Ann was in a garden like Gethsemane, dressed in a see-through white tunic, ready to be sacrificed. The sacrificer was a Jesuit priest surrounded by his aides, Roman centurions. He was standing at the edge of a well where the other sacrificial victims were "stored." Ann heard their pitiful cries from down below. They were all women, and she knew they would be dying after her.

This dream had awakened Ann in terror. It was the first time she had actually "seen" herself as a victim. The image corresponded to the feelings she had been having in her unhappy love affair, but it also brought to light in a much more general way how dangerous and despotic a certain masculine energy had become in her own psyche over the years. As she recalled this dream, I asked her to let memories come up that might be associated to the images or feelings. What she remembered immediately, to her own surprise, was how violent her father had been with her.

He had not just disappeared every night behind the paper, it turned out. Every once in a while, when he found out that Ann had behaved especially badly according to his rules, he would take off his belt and beat her. These beatings took place when Ann was between the ages of five and ten: when she stole apples from a neighbor's orchard, when she played with matches in the backyard, when she played doctor with a neighboring child.

The beatings Ann described were more than punishments. There seemed something sadistic about the controlled, livid rage she remembers in her father's face when he ordered her to undress for the beatings. Clearly, the anger and impotence he felt with his wife and his own parents came out on the rebellious daughter, the one who did what he had never dared.

These incidents did not break Ann's spirit. Her mother's contrasting encouragement of Ann's exploits, plus her own inner warrior, saw her through. But the paternal abuse, coupled with her father's frequent criticism of her—"Why don't you put on a dress like your sister?," "Why don't you study less, you might frighten the boys away?"—combined to break the link of love and trust between her and men.

As she spoke of these early memories of violence, Ann re-discovered the pain attached to them and began to realize the connection between them and some of her love affairs. She saw that she had "sought out" men such as her first husband and Robert in an attempt to re-live and repair the pain inflicted by her father. Of course, she did not seek them out consciously for this, but something in her, as in all of us, did need to go back, again and again, to try, like a child who cannot believe the emotional reality, to repair what had been broken.

She also saw that the inequalities and taboos she had experienced at home were ones she perpetuated in her adult life. The Jesuit in her dream is surrounded by Roman centurions. For Ann these figures represented "spiritual, intellectual, and temporal power in their most powerful form." Since it was taboo for her to be female, sexual, and feeling, she had espoused masculine values of power that intellectual knowledge and wisdom promised to give her. As a youngster she had never wanted to be a nun. That seemed too uninteresting. She had been fascinated, however, by the images of the Jesuits because at school she had learned that they were both "religious and smart." They also got to travel around the world and learn languages, which appealed to her. They got to live alone, in fact had to live alone, which also attracted her, having decided from the model of her parents that men and women did not go very well together.

Ann was not Catholic: her information was incomplete, which probably accounts for why she could project such idealization onto the Jesuit. As Jung has said, in the unconscious of every Catholic there is a Protestant and in the unconscious of every Protestant a Catholic. For a child who grew up with parents who were of Protestant background, but considered themselves atheists and made fun of any spiritual interest she might have, the Catholic Church with its ritual and saints seemed very appealing. Eventually she laid aside her religious interests along with other "childish" things, but the image remained in her unconscious.

The Jesuit image combined both the spiritual archetype and the father archetype in a way neither her real father nor God had been able to do. It did provide an ideal for Ann in that it gave her a human model for power, learning, and spirit to come together without the confusion of intimate relationships. Unfortunately, it also had its shadow side. Identifying with the "Jesuit" meant she had to sacrifice her womanhood. For a long time, this did not bother Ann. She would have been surprised to hear that she had done any such thing, since she had spent so much time in making herself attractive to men and in liberating herself from the conventions that had ruled her mother's life. It was only after the dream, and then in analysis, that she realized she still saw women as less important than men. Even worse was the fact that she had set herself up as the despot of her own femininity, by ignoring her feelings for so long. She had become a judgmental "Jesuit" who hated and despised the failings of "silly women who sacrifice themselves to a man." The centurions represented the armed vigilance she had employed to maintain her intellectual ascendance over the women in the well, i.e., the sensitive feminine parts of herself "stored" in the unconscious.

All this was a quite a revelation to Ann. Never before had she understood the price of her one-sidedness. The unconscious until then had been something irrelevant to her life and goals. As she pursued her analysis, however, it turned out that she had quite a rich inner life as a child. Like her father she had written poetry. She had even won a poetry contest, but her mother quickly took the credit and boasted to everyone about her smart daughter. This kind of appropriation just made Ann hide her inner life away, even from herself, until she could not ignore it any longer.

As this inner life re-awakened, she began to explore with less fear of judgment the meaning of her relationship with Peter. The word that came back again and again in connection with him was "creativity." Unlike her other lovers, Peter connected Ann both to past experiences and future possibilities. With his playful imagination and facility in a world of image, he took her back to childhood places where things were not in conflict—places she had played, games she had invented with her friends, by herself, or with her dog. Poems she had written, discoveries she had made at school, in nature—many memories of true childlike play before performance became paramount.

That part of her psyche had become taboo along with the religious feelings and feminine awareness. It was gone, over, given up along with other childlike activities. It took a taboo individual—a younger, imaginative man like Peter—to draw her away from her own ego limits and bring her across the border into the world of her forgotten, youngster self. It was as if he

Ann's Story   **155**

had entered into the psychic space of her dream of the garden of Gethsemane, walked over to the Jesuit, thumbed his nose at him, and taken Ann by the hand, saying, come on, we're going to pull all those girls out of the well and go on a picnic together. Peter played Mercury to the Jesuit's implacable Zeus-Yahweh.

Besides being mercurial and irreverent, Peter was also a Catholic. He fit right in with Ann's forgotten spiritual yearnings. She was both intrigued by his insider's easy irreverence at some of the more pompous aspects of his religion and touched by the depth of his genuine spirituality. She had never been involved with someone who took spiritual issues seriously and found herself abandoning her Jesuitical skepticism to open up to her own religious questioning.

End of Eden

As Ann described all the wonders she experienced in her encounter with Peter, it was easy to see why she felt so worried about the eventuality of losing this relationship. Everything they did when they were together seemed to release her from one more prison of the defenses she had erected against life. She even had a dream which at first seemed to confirm the perfection of their relationship.

It was another dream in a garden, but it was not a garden of death and mortification. *She dreamt that she was in a lovely sun-lit garden on the grounds of an old, beautiful mansion. Peter came and joined her, took her by the hand, and started leading her*

toward the woods that bordered the grounds. He
said he wanted to share something with her, and
she set off after him. The woods were lush, green,
dark, inviting but a little frightening.

In spite of its innocent appearance, the dream announced a change in their relationship and in Ann's
understanding of what Peter meant in her life. At first
the dream seems to be all positive. Everything is
lovely, safe, well-tended. The sun is out. There are no
ghosts or despots to spoil the scenery. Ann is alone
and in a state of contentment. The scene brings to
mind the myth of Demeter and Persephone when Persephone, the innocent daughter, was alone happily
picking flowers in the sunlight before Hades came to
take her off to another destiny.

In Ann's life at the time of the dream, she felt like
Persephone in the field. Her relationship with Peter
re-awakened the child within. Her analysis had begun
to give her enough feeling of positive mothering that
she could feel safe just to be that child, to live, to re-
capture some of the innocence of childhood that her
real experience had hardly allowed. Alas, Eden never
lasts for long.

Shortly after this dream, Ann and Peter began to
get more and more involved sexually. Their relationship lost some of its magic playfulness as they "entered
the woods" of her dream where instinctual life thrives
and the light of solar consciousness barely enters.
While still exhorting me not to tell her to stop the
relationship with Peter, she came to session after session drawn, tense, often in tears. Until then, Ann had
only feared the destruction their relationship could

cause around them, in each of their separate lives. Now as sexual passion grew, it was clear that there could be a darkness between them as well. The bliss of the beginning was turning into a nightmare of jealousy and needs.

Ann had been glad when the taboos she had put on her joyous inner child had been transgressed with Peter's aid. She was less pleased when the relationship precipitated other, more negative, parts of her psyche that had also been taboo until now.

She began to dream of tigers, of witches, of wild animals with Peter's eyes. For a while she took these images literally, as warnings of what Peter "really" was beneath his blithe and playful exterior. As her sexual passion grew, she began to feel more possessive of him. She felt devoured by her own desire and realized the tiger was not just in Peter. Meanwhile, the mature, reasoning voice inside her said that it was not his fault he could only be with her once or twice a week, but this voice made no impression on the wild animals. Ann felt sure Peter was losing interest or playing with her heart. She tortured herself with fantasies of him and his wife, him and other women, him and all the most beautiful women in the world whom he could surely have as a young man with such charm.

In fact, from what Ann described in more calm moments, he was not playing with her heart. He was genuinely in love and did not imagine a life without Ann. Still, he was also married, a father, trying to finish a university degree and earn a living all at the same time. He was as overwhelmed as she was and unable to respond to her panic and needs as often as she wanted.

In lucid moments Ann realized all this, but as difficulties in meeting times and communication grew, she saw it all as his fault and felt victimized. After all, she had risked a great deal to be with him. How could he treat her so cavalierly? This was a terrible period for Ann. All the ravenous emotional neediness she had never been allowed to feel as a child and that she had denied as an adult came to the surface. The jealousy she had felt and stifled toward her favored sister and brother, the rage she had toward her father—negative feelings never before faced erupted and claimed their due. She vacillated between anger at her lover and loathing for herself for acting "just like my mother." She felt as victimized by the intensity of her feelings as she did by her lover. For a year, she alternated between heartbreak and hope, waiting and hoping it would work out, since sometimes they still managed to re-capture the original magic and enter into that otherworldly space of creativity and joy.

After Impossible Love

With time, however, she began to accept that the price was too high. She could no longer continue to live such anguish, neglecting her work, waiting by the telephone, even driving by Peter's apartment late at night and torturing herself with images of him in bed with his wife. It wasn't that she came to her senses.

It's just that she needed to choose between passion and life, for they no longer went together. She felt sure that, if she went on, she would lose her mind, her health, or both. The impossibility was simply too much, even for the warrior heroine who had never lost a battle.

One day she arrived in my office and announced, "I have put an axe into the heart of the heroine." I found this a remarkable statement. She did not say, "I have stopped loving Peter or stopped seeing him." No, she acted on the only aspect of the relationship that she had any psychological control over, the heroine within that threatened to destroy her if she persisted. Ann gave up, and her heroine collapsed.

The relationship did not end as abruptly as her statement. It went through the separations, the reconnections, the tears, and promises that any great love puts us through as it dies to possibility. The lovers mourned together and mourned separately, but they finally parted for good. As Ann said afterwards, "We got too much into the theater. There was no place we could not go inside, but we could not find our stage outside." *This is so often the tragedy and reality of impossible love: the ground within is rich and real, but there is none without to build on in everyday life.*

Peter brought a revolution into Ann's life, opening the doors to past wounds as well as future possibilities. In spite of the pain, she did not regret their relationship. She continued in analysis and honored the revolution by exploring the chambers it had revealed in her psyche. She made some peace with childhood traumas. Even more important, she continued to deepen her connection with the inner life of image and symbol that her impossible love had revived.

Among other things, she realized that the warrior heroine she had tried to kill should not entirely disappear after all. The psychic energy carried by this inner figure was not just destructive. It had simply become too dominant, pushing aside other inner selves that wanted to live as well. Ann learned to dialogue with this heroine when she felt caught by her blind, self-righteous energy. She also learned to dialogue with other figures as they came up in dreams or spoke through her emotions. The sense of theater that had attracted her so much to Peter became a living reality, as she let go into the "play" of the psyche.

On the outside, there were no radical changes. She did not quit her job, don dungarees, and head for the woods to commune with nature. What had changed was that she no longer needed to compete and prove herself all the time. She received tenure, but it did not give her the victorious "I'll show you all" feeling she had anticipated. On the contrary, it allowed her the peace of mind that permitted her to plunge into her work with renewed interest. It also provided a sense of security for the first time in her life, a feeling that Ann had never allowed herself before. The word "security" had always been associated with images of stagnation and complacency, a reflection of her parents' unhappy lives.

At this point in her life, however, Ann could stop reacting to her parents. With two good friends, she

Ann's Story   *161*

bought a triplex apartment and set about making it into a home. During this time she came into analysis one day and said that she had read a sentence in a book that had impressed her very much. It was a book by a Jungian analyst, Murray Stein, on mid-life. To paraphrase her quote, the sentence was "the mid-life crisis signals the end of endless potential." Reading this brought a flood of relief to Ann. Rather than hear in these words a condemnation and end, she heard the permission to stop thinking she had to go farther, farther, higher, higher all the time. They were confirmation of the process she had already begun. She could stop and listen to the birds, write poetry, renovate her house, prepare her courses, compete when she felt like it, but not out of compulsion. She was allowed to come home.

These changes, though subtle, were very profound. Yet there is no absolute happy ending to Ann's story. Like most people she continued to live ups and downs. In the time I knew her she did not fall in love again, impossibly or possibly. The man of every woman's dreams did not appear in her life to reward her for the work she had done on herself. The revolution brought to Ann's life by impossible love did not end in happiness forever after. That only happens in fairy tales, and Ann was only too grateful to have left the fairy-tale illusions of her inner wounded child. What her "wrong" relationship accomplished was a breaking down of psychic barriers that had kept her from living, putting her into a more genuine relationship with herself and the world outside.

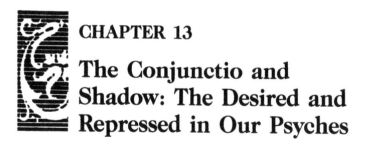

CHAPTER 13

The Conjunctio and Shadow: The Desired and Repressed in Our Psyches

Through Ann's story we have seen that we must make certain links to the past if impossible love is not to propel us into a series of "repetition compulsions." If we do not know our histories, we have no say in our futures. Her story offers one example of the myriad elements that form the fabric of our history, creating patterns we don't even know are there until we pick the material up. Every person who goes through an impossible love will find patterns woven by his or her individual experiences and emotional lacunas. Robert Stein underlines the importance of this return to the past when he says, "There is no possibility for fulfilling the soul's desire for union until the child is transformed and healed. Its neglected and abused nature must be attended to before it becomes capable of loving. . . ."[1]

When we fall into passion, however, we are adults. Part of the very confusion that passion brings is the conflict between the needs of the "children" involved and those of the adults. The meeting of lovers in an impossible love is not only an attempt of the psyche to repair the wounds of the past. As adults in love we

have also to contend with the contents of our unconscious in the here and now, as they erupt into our lives
under the influence of passion. Just as the archetypal
force of love leads us to transgress our own taboos,
so does it bring us into an encounter with other archetypal motifs that are colored by our childhood experience but not solely determined by it. These motifs,
in fact, lead away from our past and our particular ego-
bound identity. "The deepest need of the soul in any
human relationship is never therapeutic, it is the desire to unite with another."[2]

This Other is many-faced. It is impossible to know
in the time of passion whether the Other is outside
or in, flesh or spirit. Union with our own soul or with
our lover. We are captivated by archetypes that emerge
simultaneously and claim us in different ways—the
Conjunctio and the Shadow, blissful union and unwelcome dissension. Each archetype demands our attention if we are to engage in the "soul work" that
Hillman refers to when he says that "all impossible
loves force upon us a discipline of interiorizing."[3]

The Conjunctio

The Conjunctio, or Union of Opposites, is an image that has fascinated mankind and womankind since
the beginning of history. Feeling themselves in exile
from original Oneness, humans have always conceived
of a Perfect Union of opposites in an ideal sphere. Yin
and Yang, Sol and Luna, Heaven and Earth, King and
Queen, Matter and Spirit are but a few of the dualities

imagined as opposites in search of union and reconciliation. The Heavenly Marriage, the Philosopher's Stone, the Opus, the Golden Flower—various metaphors express the goal of this universal human striving. Myths that depict male and female, gods and goddesses coming together in perfect oneness existed long before the notion of romantic love in the West. The basic symbolism of such a recurring image revolves around creativity. When opposites unite, something new is born.

On a strictly biological level this is obvious. Aphrodite and her love-goddess counterparts in other cultures were indeed worshiped for their generating powers. By joining with her male partners and putting men and women under her intoxicating spell of sexual attraction, Aphrodite ensured the continuity of the species—creativity as procreation.

But the image of Masculine and Feminine joined together in love and creative energy carries far more meaning than the purely biological one. It is a symbol of transformative possibilities that lures us into creative enterprise. In those rare moments when we truly live creatively, we are blessed by the archetype of the Conjunctio and briefly experience what it is like when all our conflicting energies work together. No matter how cynical we may be about religion, myth, or even love, we all carry a deep longing within for these moments of perfect union.

Unfortunately, in our culture the Conjunctio as a guiding ideal has been almost exclusively relegated to the sphere of romantic love. Our religion does not give us a picture of masculine and feminine creatively interacting. We have too few alchemists, animists, or story tellers to keep the conjunctio image alive in other forms than the purely personal one of human men and women. Only our dreams still speak in metaphorical language of union and separation as psychological realities. Even here, however, we tend to single out the masculine and feminine figures as the main carriers of opposites needing reconciliation. Mother, Father, animus, anima forever spinning around as we search for union within and love without.

But behind our obsession with love lie spiritual and psychological yearnings that can never be satisfied with an ordinary mortal. In spite of all our psychological knowledge and despite the social freedoms we have to find a partner in almost any milieu, love has not become any more possible than it has ever been. Little has changed since the time of Heloïse and Abelard. On the contrary, as we have seen, people still gravitate as much, if not more, to the wrong kinds of love, and this is not solely because of unresolved childhood issues.

What has changed is that love is more in demand than ever before. If we allow that behind this demand there are spiritual and emotional longings that are often more urgent than needs for intimacy and shared family life, then it is not surprising there are so many impossible loves. Nor is it surprising that these loves should take us so far out of ordinary life. That seems to be exactly their purpose. As we saw with Abelard and Heloïse, Ann and Peter, and others, impossible love creates an opportunity for many opposites to come together that had been separated and forbidden before: young and old, naive and experienced, strong and weak, intellectual and emotional, spiritual and sensual, past and present, present and future. From the meeting and collision of all these energies in the lovers' lives, something new emerges that is not the result of biology, hormones, or honeymoons. The marriage takes place within.

How Can Marriage Happen Inside?

I first heard the expression "inner marriage" in Zürich when I was in training to become an analyst. For years I had heard of and read about the inner union of animus and anima that should be sought by all those who undertake an analysis. Every time a love problem came up, mine or someone else's, some analytical authority always responded by pointing out that the "real" problem was inside. Love was a question of projection—we needed to withdraw those projections and get on our individuated way with a more integrated attitude, which would result from our Work on the Opposites within. If we did it right, we would enter into the elect circle of the initiated who had celebrated the heavenly marriage in their own psyches. Love on the outside would then be irrelevant or happen without problems. Actually, it was unclear what the prognosis was in practical terms.

At the time I was torn between two opposing responses to this idea. Sometimes I believed it. It resonated in my soul, and I was sure if I had enough hours of analysis I would come to know the truth of this inner union. At other times, I thought it a completely ridiculous idea. It seemed like a kind of psychological blackmail akin to church dogma—love is not of this life and flesh, go inside and find it where it belongs, i.e., in psyche and dreams.

Today, I think I misunderstood the meaning of the "conjunctio" archetype that appeared so tantalizing and yet difficult to grasp. I think both my responses were wrong and both my responses were right. There is such a thing as an inner sense of union. It is not based uniquely on a static image of masculine and feminine energies within coming together in one final embrace. It is not a loftier level of love that supercedes the real life messes of attraction between the sexes. Rather, it is a result of living such messes. At the same time, paradoxically, it makes them easier to live. In other words, a feeling of being centered, or in union or harmony, does increase as we lose our childhood illusions, our False Selves, and our other defenses. As it increases, we feel much less thrown off-balance by life's upsets and challenges. But the movement is a two-way street. The more we accept the experiences life brings, work on them, make them part of our beings, the more balanced we end up feeling.

The inner marriage results when we allow the contradictions in our psyches to meet in various degrees of harmony and discord. This does not mean that these forces always end up creating something new. Like any marriage, an inner one has its bad moments, when no one in our psyche gets along with anyone else. Mind fights body and heart goes on strike. What matters, however, is that the flow is more often open than blocked. The "circulatio" between unconscious and conscious, ego and shadow brings more life than when one of them goes it alone.

This is one of the gifts an impossible love can make to us. The "conjunctio" that cannot take place outside looks for and finds another fulfillment within. Along with the painful loss of outer hopes come discoveries of inner realities as we encounter the "others" within. We have seen some of these others already in reference to figures from our personal past. We have made allusions to the discovery in the unconscious of spiritual yearning and creativity. What remains to be explored more closely in the psychological realm is the archetype of the Shadow, for it underpins all the others.

Shadow: The Unloved Inside

Shadow, in Jung's shortest and most direct definition, is "the thing or person we have no wish to be...."[4] In personal life, it is the part of our personality we have had to repress in order to be acceptable in our milieu. In this sense, it is composed of all that is split-off when only the False Self, or adapted part of ourselves, is allowed to live. Hidden in the darkness of our unconscious lie anger, greed, sadness, desire, neediness, ambition, and even creativity—negative and not so negative split-off parts. Early on, any expression of these feelings was frowned upon, so we learned to keep them out of sight. Eventually, however, we need to retrieve them if we are to become fully alive.

A typical example of such emotions rising to the surface in negative form was when Ann found herself overwhelmed by possessiveness, loss of control, and sexual jealousy with Peter. Such shameful feelings not only jarred with her image of herself but also made her realize the connection with her mother, who had lived out these undesirable traits so much that Ann had completely banned any awareness of them in her adult personality.

Yet, Ann's mother also had an instinctual warmth and enthusiasm that her father lacked. Ann's finding herself acting like her mother, though horrifying at first, allowed her to open up to the maternal heritage and be glad of the healthy energy it offered her. Often the negative energies that come out of our shadow when we are in the throes of impossible love may be just what we need to re-discover links with our psychological inheritance. Though the parent may have expressed these energies in unpalatable ways, in and of themselves they have no negative value. Like the color of our eyes, they are part of the genetic pool we descend from. If we cut them off completely, we lose part of our own substance.

A man, for instance, who led a sophisticated, urbane life as a city yuppie in rejection of his uncouth backwoods family, and especially of his father, found himself obsessed with sex when he fell in love with a young soccer player. Suddenly, all the instinctual behavior he had despised in his father came back to haunt him in the form of his unbridled sexual desire. No physical degradation was too much to accept at the hands of his lover. Only when he had fallen into this for some time did he realize that such an invasion of erotic energy re-connected him with the father he had loathed. Then he could see that, in cutting his father out of his life, he had also rejected his own instinctual needs, fleeing into over-refinement that gave expression only to the "higher" parts of his being.

Constantly impossible passion confronts us with that which we have neglected, denied, or forsworn. When it doesn't do so by overwhelming us with our own craziness, it does so by pairing us with individuals who, to our conscious minds, appear to be "impossible." *In falling in love with the wrong person, we fall in love with shadow, our own unlived life.* Since unconscious contents in our psyches generally appear in someone else first, we do not immediately recognize this. We are so shocked by the wrongness of our choice of lover or entranced by the magic of it all that we are not able to see the inner correspondences.

Projection of the "Wrong" onto Another Person

Yet, whatever belongs to us psychologically and goes unclaimed in our conscious life will sooner or later appear in the form of another individual. Projection precedes insight. Many individuals may annoy us or leave us indifferent, but when someone drives us to distraction, it is because they have touched on shadow. Generally they express or do something out-right that we have forbidden ourselves to even think of. It just isn't a possibility in our inner world of values. For example, a colleague who seriously gets on our nerves because of her whininess may reflect to us that we have put overly strict limits on our own expression of vulnerability. Something in us finds it unbearable when another person lets himself go into behaviors we have forbidden to ourselves. Usually, however, we do not identify the psychological content. We simply react emotionally to that individual as if she were the problem.

When the person who carries shadow for us is our partner in an impossible love, then he or she surely carries aspects of ourselves that are even more unconscious than usual, aspects we had consigned to the unconscious as taboo. Such unconscious contents remain both fascinating and terrifying, which is one of the reasons that we find ourselves loving and fearing in such extremely wrong relationships. *What attracts us in the outer love relationship reflects all we fear and need to love within.* For example, a patient who falls in love with a therapist may be irresistibly attracted to the authority, strength, and insight she or he does not dare own. A therapist who falls in love with a patient may be moved by the neediness, vulnerability, and inner child she has not allowed herself to live since donning the responsible robes of the healer.

Usually, under the influence of passion, we enter into the illusion that with this person we are in contact with something completely new, an unknown world, a foreign land both intriguing and slightly scary. We would say to ourselves at this time that there is no way I "really" have or need the particular traits of this partner in impossible love. Ann would have said this about Peter. Yet after their relationship, she became more playful and imaginative. Heloïse would have said the same about Abelard, and after their passion she became an intellectual leader in her own right. A brilliant man who once fell in love with a rather stupid woman threw his head back in surprise when I suggested she carried the value of stupidity that he needed to allow himself more of. Years later, when I next met him, he admitted that, in the time following the relationship with her, he had begun to find "something beautiful in stupidity." His need to be brilliant and trenchant at all times had been tempered by the pleasure of being foolish and even ignorant on occasion.

It is always dangerous to live with the illusion that one is the role one plays, dangerous to think that we are just one thing, a simple, uncomplicated human being with a clear social identity. No one is so simple, and impossible love comes into our lives to confirm this.

Mutual Effects, Opposite Results When Shadows Meet in Love

Because of this reciprocal meeting of shadow between the two lovers, the relationship may have the opposite effect on each. The outer inequality changes as each opens up taboo areas for the other. The stronger, older, or richer one will descend from her pedestal to play and be passionate. The weaker, younger, or poorer one will go up—into all the dignity, confidence, and authority he had not dared take on before. In a way, the weaker member carries the strength and vision of the unconscious. Confident that the stronger partner will be able to take care of him or herself, the weaker one is less hampered by feelings of responsibility regarding the other's vulnerability and more free to act and speak from passion rather than from convention. In his or her greater innocence, he or she speaks with the mouth of a babe, directly from the heart, and from the present moment with fewer of the encumbrances of duty and reputation at stake for the stronger one. As with Heloïse, one's love bestows an assurance and new sense of specialness that is difficult to resist. It puts one into the center of a crusade in which one is both leader and soldier all at the same time. Unafraid of what people will think or the lost reputation and position, one will vanquish the taboos, the hypocrisy, the obstacles. One has found a cause greater than oneself to serve, and any protestation or argument just becomes another provocation.

For the other lover, the apparently stronger one, this language is very seductive. Very often, he or she has lost touch with the inner child and has been cut off from that space where everything, including play, is both meaningful and "free." Often nothing in his life is free anymore, in the sense of total spontaneity and involvement. She is caught in her own identification with a super-ego set of values, and when the Other comes in with a message that these values don't count nearly as much as those of the heart, she is all too ready to listen.

Conscious and unconscious, super-ego and shadow collide in love and fear. Each lover will be grateful to the other for opening the doors into forbidden parts of his or her own psyche, and at the same time fearful of claiming these forbidden parts. In impossible love we recognize the other as our other half, our soul-mate. The Conjunctio calls. But this insistent feeling of belonging together is agonizingly difficult to build on because half of it is always in the unconscious or carried by the other person. A dialogue between ego and shadow of one of the lovers would go like this:

I am your shadow. You recognize me, yet you are afraid to claim me openly. I have much to bring you, if you would only embrace me.

You are my shadow. I want you, and yet my ego needs to resist. Only in the moments of passion can I surrender myself to that which I have always refused.

Shadow as Ideal

As we follow the dark night of our own soul through the vagaries of impossible love, we meet many others within. Some of these others are negative, but not all. As we have seen from examples above, much of what we call shadow is in fact repressed light.

Shadow is not just what a person does not want to be. It is also what a person does not *dare* to be.

This observation takes us into the final section on shadow in impossible love, which touches on the strange play of idealization and envy that is so often present in such relationships. We have seen in previous chapters how each partner idealizes the other to the point of turning one another into deities. What is the meaning of such idealizing? Is it just idolatry leading to a magical mystery trip, or is there something else involved?

On the one hand, the incredibly stubborn idealization that attaches itself to the lover in passionate love points to the archetype of the conjunctio that we have discussed before. It expresses the deep human need for an image of spiritual energies joining together in cosmic creativity. Frustrated in this search by an a-religious society, the psyche of many individuals . naturally turns to the human love relationship as a way of experiencing the Heavenly Marriage.

On the other hand, and on a more mundane level, people need to have ideals in everyday life. They are vital to mental health. Children need ideals to reach for that lead them into the future. But adults need them too. As Margarete Mitscherlich says in her book *La Femme Pacifique*, we all need to be able "to dream the future which is not just a fact of youth, but also the necessary condition of creativity and renewal in adult life as well."[5]

Having no ideals at all leaves an individual in a cut-off state of emptiness, apathy, and depression. Being exposed to ideals that are absurdly out of reach, such as the models proposed by popular media, is no better. It just creates a state of impotent envy and anger, whose results we see every day in the culture of violence and material inequality. In impossible love there is a delicate balance between ideal and envy that can turn purely destructive or become a force for "dreaming the future." To understand where the ideals are pointing, we need to ask whose future we are dreaming about and what ideals belong to whom.

This is not an easy thing to do. Just as it is difficult to separate what shadow belongs to our lover, what to ourselves, and what to the relationship itself, so is it very hard to discern the reality behind our idealizations. Our partner seems to be so different in his or her gifts. It is possible to get stuck in the other's aura and never connect it to our own psyches. The other's glib charm, perfect self-assurance, daring madness, or heart-breaking sensitivity doesn't seem to have anything to do with us, and we don't have a clue how to connect what we adore out there and what we need in here.

One of the most helpful ways to focus this search is through ideal's darker relative, envy. When I asked a woman who was madly and hopelessly in love with a very introverted, undemonstrative man what she idealized most in him, she had trouble answering. She could only speak of the irresistible attraction to his stoicism and integrity. These indeed were objective qualities he probably had, but naming them did not advance our conversation very much. Lots of people have these qualities, and there was nothing in her response that made an apparent link between them and her own personality.

When I asked, however, what do you most *envy* in X, she had no trouble. The words tumbled out quickly and fluently, "I envy his damned ability to never over-react, to always keep a lid on and never lose his cool, to arrange his life so that he is never compromised by too many relationships and too many material responsibilities, his ability to be satisfied with a minimum."

Well, that was much more precise and much more revealing. Here, in her very frustration with him, we also find her envy. Outwardly, she kept hoping he would become more like her, more expressive and talkative and generous with feeling and energy and money and time. But inwardly, she envied his ability not to be so. From this, it is not hard to hypothesize that she needed in fact more of these very qualities. Like many women, she was constantly over-extended in time and energy, constantly worried about not being generous enough with her friends and colleagues. Underneath, it was clear too that such generosity was also related to a certain grandiosity, a conviction that she could do it all, be it all, solve it all. Her passion for such a "minimalist" lover showed her that she had been woefully lacking in the discipline and humility needed to reduce her need for extravagant show and accomplishment. In addition, she realized how much this had worked against her other needs—needs for more time alone, for less outer responsibility, and more focus on her personal creativity and interests which never got off the ground because there was always something else to do or prove. This was quite a blow to her pride. She had been convinced that her generosity was one of her best traits—she had not recognized the grandiosity that lay behind it and how it led her to betray other parts of herself.

Their love affair did not turn out to be possible because of her insight. On the contrary, understanding more of what her lover expressed and that she had repressed, she was able to start reducing her extroverted activities and to find real pleasure in a less extravagant way of life. She also realized in doing this that, though she still felt love for him, she was no longer so fascinated by his silence and control, and no longer desirous to be the one who broke through his armor, as she had been compulsively trying to do for several years. He no longer seemed an invincible, unattainable being who "had" something she needed to hold on to. Through her envy, she had touched her own wound—the imbalance and forced hyperactivity she had adopted long ago to please her environment and to give herself a social identity she felt secure behind. As she took back her own destiny, she let him go on to his.

Other individuals speak of envying the "free spirit" of their lover, or the "blithe unconsciousness," or the ability to "selfishly concentrate" on something, no matter what. What we envy tells us what we need to learn more about for ourselves. In fact, all love, impossible or not, contains elements of envy and ideal because we never love only out of what we already have. Love of any kind "flows more readily from weakness and psychopathologies than from strength."[6] Envy and shadow in impossible love can help us identify just what these weaknesses are and what we need to own, rather than resent, in the other, in order to get on with our dreams.

In the next and final chapter, we will look at the dream of love in a less personal fashion, following our lovers of today as they join the collectivity of other lovers from other centuries into the Mystery of Amor.

PART V

The Mystery of Amor

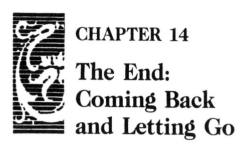

CHAPTER 14

The End:
Coming Back
and Letting Go

The Infernal Couple: Lovers of the Work

Every Love is a revolution in that genuine love always brings about deep change. Much of what I have said in this book about impossible love would be true for possible love as well. The differences are ones of degree, but they are very important. The efforts we make to grow and change in ordinary love (as if any love were ordinary) may lead to creativity and self-knowledge, just as they do in impossible love. But this initiation uses reality as its terrain and possibility as its incentive. The initiation by impossible love, on the contrary, goes by way of another path and takes us to a different kind of union.

Other cultures have recognized this difference in emphasis. In Greece there were temples to Hera, the goddess of marriage, and temples to Aphrodite, the goddess of love. Each goddess had her domain. The Greeks recognized that love was not just one thing to be expressed in one way. They acknowledged that sexual love between adults could have different forms and different purposes. What mattered above all was to honor the sacred aspect of each. Love was never just this or just that. The gods were potentially present in every carnal union.

We do not have such temples today. We have only the sacred "temple" of marriage, or coupledom, and the profane areas of everything else. Sexuality, pornography, erotic passion, neurotic affairs, impossible love are all put into the same bin outside of the temple walls of healthy relationship. Once, long ago, we did have another, more interesting way to conceive of other kinds of sexual love. In our own European culture, there was a brief moment when love outside of consecrated relationship was deemed the most desirable of all.

Beginning in the eleventh century and blossoming through the twelfth, the Courts of Love of what would later be France invented a "code d'amor" that attempted to change our ideas of love in the Western world. In these Courts of Love, unmarried pairs of lovers, knights and ladies, pledged to follow together the code d'amor and to study treatises on the art of loving—*l'Arte Amandi*—as a means to spiritual transcendence. The goal was never marriage and children, or even pleasure for its own sake. The goal was to cultivate the intensity of passion as a way of going beyond one's selfhood. It was a kind of Western love yoga in which desire of the senses and desire of the soul were joined in order to re-create "that moment at the dawn of time when the opposites were not yet in contradiction."[1] It was a metaphysical and theological realization of the Conjunctio.

The couples who participated in these Courts of

Love were subjected to strict protocol and judged— hence the label of Courts—by a group of ladies as to how well they submitted to the difficult discipline of using physical desire as a trampoline to a higher plane of consciousness. A pair of lovers was called the "Infernal Couple" because their passion took place outside of the sacrament of marriage. In the world at large, they would have been condemned to hell for such an affront to normal rules. But in the intimate world of the Courts of Love, they were the carriers of new values, imposed by the ladies, not the knights. For the first time, and for a very brief time, feminine values reigned between men and women, values in which body and spirit were not separated, but joined together in sexual love.[2]

Infernal in the context of the Courts of Love came to mean, therefore, not hell-bound, but outside of the ordinary and orthodox. The couples' unmarried state was officially "wrong," yet it was indispensable to the Work. Married couples could not participate because their love, if love there was, had other goals, procreative and economic ones, not spiritual ones.

Today's Infernal Couples do not have access to Courts of Love or spiritual values that give deeper meaning to impossible love. We have manuals and videos on sex, and books on relationships, but we have no code d'amor to guide us through passion and reconnect it with the sacred. The Courts of Love have been forgotten, their message appropriated and distorted by the centuries that followed. Little by little, romantic love has been turned into an aesthetic tradition and a commercial goldmine. It has lost its original focus in which discipline and passion came together in an *unsentimental* psychic container called romantic love, discipline that led away from everyday reality and toward the godhead.

Yet, even without this recognized ideal, we somehow know, when we are carried away by the force of impossible love, that we are involved in a Great Work. The fact is that an impossible love, more than any other, puts us to work, and this on many levels. We go into therapy looking for answers, we consult our friends to see what they think, we read books, wait for a phone call, plan new strategies, mobilize our forces as never before to endure and overcome. And all the while we sense that no matter how much we learn about relationships, how much we need to understand about our childhoods, how much progress we make with our lover, we will never find an answer that explains it all. There is a Court of Love within that says, "this, your impossible love, is more than just a hang-up. It is an initiation."

The Mysteries:
Initiation of an Asymmetrical Two

We have seen the effects of impossible love on our self-awareness and on our awareness of other levels of existence. In impossible love we are all Infernal Couples. At the same time, through this initiatory process we re-connect with the tradition of the Great Mystery Cults of pagan times.

In these cults, individuals were initiated into the

underworld in order to enter into new dimensions of reality, especially the reality of death as another form of being. As they followed the ritual that led down to the underworld and back again, initiates encountered the gods of the realm of darkness. When they returned above ground, their eyes saw the world differently. Just like people who describe near-death experiences today, the individuals who undertook the voyage to the underworld often emerged with a feeling of being reborn through their encounter with the Dark Ones.

Impossible love may be just such a voyage. It always goes toward death—death of an old attitude, death of innocence about ourselves and the world. What is more, like nearly all the Mystery cults, it leads there by means of a descent of two together. As Hillman points out, "The initiation through the Mighty Ones is an initiation of the Two and an asymmetrical two."3

Now we begin to see the necessity of the inequality and verticality that are such constants in impossible love. Religious initiation always proceeded by the pairing of unequals—old/young, wise/naive, immortal/mortal, ordained/novice. Whether we refer to the great Feminine Mysteries of Mother/Daughter, Demeter and Persephone in Eleusis, or the much later descent of the Christian, Dante, into the seven circles of hell guided by the Pagan, Virgil, we find ourselves in the presence of an asymmetrical two. The very lack of match between them creates the dynamism that leads to new consciousness. Who leads above will be led below. Each member of the pair has something to give to the other, and the imbalance that is so frustrating in ordinary life turns out to be the key to otherworldly experience.

In impossible love, this imbalance makes us fall down, down, into an underworld where joy and death meet simultaneously, as they only can in myth and mystic experience. Later, like the initiates of old returning from the depths, we may emerge from an impossible love with our consciousness transformed. Paradoxically, the splitting we so deplored forces us to question our idea of oneness as an indivisible unity and to find wholeness in a new and "dual structure of consciousness"[4] in which our humanity and divinity meet and acknowledge each other.

Throughout our wrong love we have felt alternately very flesh-and-blood real and very ephemerally unreal. We have been lusty and animal in our desire, and then disincarnated and holy in our love. By the end, we are obliged to bow to the evidence that we are all of these and more. We can no longer claim innocence about the others who inhabit our psychic houses. We are capable of the best and the worst, of great truth and great lies, of great generosity and great pettiness, like all human beings. But most of all, in the Mystery of Amor, we are just initiates, not conductors. We can say no or we can say yes. The gods will do the rest.

The Return:
Can the Impossible Become Possible?

Unlike the modern mystery stories that sell so well today, the Mystery of impossible love has no "solution." There is no magic formula to extract it from our hearts and wrap things up neatly. There is, however, a resolution, or a denouement, a time when the voyage must end. For most people, this denouement unfolds as the lovers make the return trip up from their shared underworld descent and back into their separate everyday lives. I will describe some of the principal milestones of this trip further on. First of all, let us look at a few other ways in which an impossible love could end.

One way would be for it to become possible. Many people have asked me if this could ever happen. I wish I could give a definite answer, but I cannot. I can only say that sometimes it happens, but most of the time it doesn't. When it does happen, however, the basic itinerary for the lovers will be the same as it is for those who complete their voyage together and then go their separate ways. In other words, in order for the impossible to turn into possible human relationship, the lovers must leave the container of the sublime, the temple of Aphrodite. Sometimes the shift can be made. It is the normal movement when infatuation and in-loveness lead to more realistic love.

But impossible love as I have been describing it is not infatuation. It is passion at its most intense, involving people who have much that separates them in the outer world. If they are at their most alive in the moments when they unite, despite their wrongness for each other, then it is unlikely they will survive a right kind of union. They are not just visitors to Aphrodite's temple, they are devotees of her Mystery together. To use the language of the Courts of Love, the Infernal Couple did not end up marrying each other.

Then, people ask, can we at least be friends after our shared initiation? To this I would answer, yes, and probably more easily than becoming possible lovers. But again, for this to happen, there must be time in between. We cannot just jump from the energy of one archetype into that of another. The container of passion must be closed, and the ashes cold, before the eros of friendship can replace the "amor" of passion.

The Return: Non-Resolution

Another way that impossible love may end is in a non-resolution. A person may live a passion that is so disturbing to her consciousness she represses or denies it afterwards and puts all her energy into restoring her public persona to what it was before. In this case, the message is lost. There is no integration, no deepening.

Yet another possibility of non-assimilation comes from the opposite pole. As an acquaintance of mine and a veteran of several impossible loves put it, "I think I prefer the mystic experience of passion and impossibility to the other kind of love. *My friends are life. My lovers are death. And I need both."* This person is not a groupie or a Peter Pan in search of constant flights from daily reality. He is an extremely hardworking, creative individual in his own right, and I found it important to take his reflection into account, for I realized as he spoke that this was also a valid choice. His involvement with passionate, impossible love keeps him in contact with the extremes of his inner nature and his creativity, and he is honest enough to see that this kind of involvement is more important to him than the security of a calmer, more "real" love life. The important thing, I think, is choice. Knowing what you are doing and taking a stand for it. No one can say whether another should or should not give up an impossible love affair. We can only attempt to know for ourselves what we are living and decide to embrace it and go on, or stop and retreat.

Resolution and Return

At some point, however, for those who stay in, the passion itself will lead to a desire for resolution. The intensity cannot be maintained forever, it is exhausting and time-consuming, and eventually it collides too much with other values in our lives that claim their due as well. This collision may be precipitated by outer interference—the lovers are separated, someone denounces them, etc.—or inner tensions—the anguish is too great, the price too high. Whatever the cause, it usually signals the point at which the destructive side has begun to increase, and the creative energy to decrease, when pain and darkness threaten to submerge the joy and ecstasy completely. In fairy tales and legends, the problem of resolution is solved naturally by the death of the lovers before their own shadow takes over. But in real life, it is not so simple. To literally die or kill from passion is to miss the point, betraying both love and death.

If we are to both live and be up to the *tremendum* of passion, we must find another way to go. Fortunately, we are not alone. Our own psyches will help us if we will only listen. When it is time to leave the otherworldly spheres of impossible love, we usually find ourselves feeling more and more negative about it. When it is time for separation, nature steps in and generates anger, disillusionment, bitterness, fatigue, hurt, all things that make us feel we can no longer continue. Whereas before, the negative feelings seemed absolutely cosmic, and we were involved in a battle of Good and Evil, Us and Them, Gods and Devils, Above and Below, later these negative voices become far more human. They speak of weariness and disappointment and humiliation, and help prepare us to leave the Land of the Chosen in order to return to the rest of our lives. Like the participants in the Mysteries, we must at some point turn around and start the trip back. If not, the very place that has transformed our being and connected us to our spiritual selves will become our tomb. We will drown in the unconscious and never bring back what we have experienced. There will be no enrichment, only loss of soul.

Sacrifice and Surrender

Lassitude, despair, simply running out of energy are all part of the return trip. The moments of joy are shorter and shorter, even the memories of joy pale beside the recall of humiliation, and all this signals the End. This happens naturally. We don't have to generate it and we cannot stop it. There is just one thing we can do to help the process a little, and that is to let go, to make a sacrifice, not of our love, but of our control.

This is exactly what Heloïse could not do, but she had no other life to return to. She had only the convent to live in and her love for Abelard to live for. Because of this she held on to her impossible love and, fortunately for us, expressed its truth in words that echo down the centuries.

Most of us, however, are not Heloïses. We may love as she did, but we usually have lives more like Abelard's, with demands and challenges and activities that require our attention and call us away from impossible love's closed vessel. We need to be able to give up, surrender, before passion turns into purely destructive tragedy.

To sacrifice, however, does not mean to throw away, deny, or get rid of. It does not imply a garage sale of the psyche. The word itself means to "make sacred," so the gesture of sacrifice implies offering something up to the gods in order for them to transform it onto a higher level.[5] A lamb is sacrificed so that the gift of its body will be received on high and transmuted into positive spiritual energies. These in turn will come back to earth in the form of benevolent weather and ensure a good harvest the following year. What is sacrificed is never junk. It is always the best, for only the dearest deserves to be offered and transformed.

In our consumer society where we throw away or replace with never a thought for the source, we have lost the meaning of the sacrifice, as well as the ritual. Yet we know instinctively that we need to let go in order for certain things to happen. We need to give up the psychological defenses that we have loved and needed, if we are going to live more fully, but in the giving, we do not deny or crush them. When we are ready, we start, gradually, to let them go. Little by little we stop trying to tame our psyche as if it were a wild beast and allow ourselves to listen and relate to it instead. In exchange, it begins to relate back to us. For example, we learn to listen to our anxiety instead of trying to eliminate it by pill and by will, and we discover that, if we listen long enough, it will lead us to a vital message about our real needs and experience. To do this we have had to sacrifice our ego control and willpower. Whenever we are brought to an impasse in life, there is usually something that must be sacrificed in order for things to start flowing once again. Old ways must constantly be sacrificed in order for their energy to be transformed into new ones.

The situation in impossible love is no exception. When we are at the point where there is no more life in the love, no more vivifying challenge and effort, only bitterness and martyrdom, then it is time to let go. To sacrifice, *not the love itself*, but the impossible passion and the hope that we can make it, force it, to be possible. We need to do what Ann did when she put an axe into her heroine—to cease our heroic attempts to force the situation, change the other or ourselves, blame the other or ourselves. Our attempts to try one more tactic, adopt one more winning attitude—all these must be sacrificed, but not the love. The love needs to be kept and honored. It is the hard-won treasure brought back from the depths, the seed of future love and creativity. It is vital, therefore, not to leave the *experience of loving* behind, for even though we cannot hold on to the Other and make our impossible love into a real-life partnership, our capacity for love will have nonetheless deepened through our otherworldly initiation. Finally, although it may sound outrageous, especially when the bitterness and pain are fresh, we need one day, perhaps a long, long time in the future, to be grateful to that Other who, perhaps all unwittingly, accompanied us into the Mysteries, as the other half of an Infernal Couple.

Incurable Longing

There is no cure for impossible love when it revolutionizes our lives. When it leads to the future as well as into the past, when it cannot be comprehended on a purely personal level, then it is not an illness, but an initiation. Initiation into depths, but also into longing, and this will not, should not, ever cease. Somehow our longing keeps us in contact with that "dual structure of consciousness" mentioned before. As creatures of earth, we seem to need a promised land or a lost paradise, something behind and something ahead that we can never quite get hold of. It is the ideal I spoke of in previous chapters that we need in order to go toward our dreams. But it is more than that. We need not only attainable ideals to work toward, but also unattainable ones. We need to believe there is something beyond our horizon, and today horizons are less and less out there in new countries to conquer, and more and more in here, in our own unexplored psyches. As Hillman notes in "Pothos," "There is a kind of love that is neither lust nor relationship, but longing for the unattainable that is never satisfied by the actual possession of the object."[6]

This longing keeps us in proximity to our souls. It reminds us, as we conscientiously go through the obligations and activities of every day, that there is a place, a "somewhere else" where we also belong and need to go to from time to time. We are reminded of this place by a song we hear on the radio, a sentence we read in a newspaper, a picture on a subway wall, a memory brought to life by a smell. We usually associate this longing with the human object of our impossible loving, but such reminders may also evoke a time—a year of happiness long forgotten—or a place—a country loved and left—or an activity—music embraced and then given up. In fact, when we can actually go to that place, do that activity, re-create all the elements of that happy time, we find that it's not that either. Even if an impossible love becomes possible, our longing will still be there. It will simply change form, reminding us that we are never quite all here and that part of us always belongs to an Other.

Notes

Introduction

1. Josephine Hart, *Damage*, p. 200.

Chapter 1

1. All quotations from Abelard or Heloïse are taken from the letters they exchanged—either the "Love Letters" ("Lettres D'Amour") or "Letters of Direction" ("Lettres de Direction")—or from Abelard's "Letter to a Friend or Story of My Calamities" ("Lettre a Un Ami ou Recit de Mes Malheurs"). These documents are published in *Lettres D'Heloïse et D'Abelard* (Geneva: La Guilde du Livre et Clairefontaine, 1970). The translations from the French are mine.
2. Joseph Campbell, *Creative Mythology*, p. 178.
3. Ibid.

Chapter 2

1. *Encyclopedia Britannica*, Macropedia, vol. I, pp. 10–11. All biographical information, apart from Abelard's own words, is taken from this source.

2. Abelard, "Letter to a Friend," p. 32.
3. *Encyclopedia Britannica*, Micropedia, vol. IV, p. 1008. All information on Heloïse's biography, apart from her own telling and Abelard's remarks, is taken from this source.
4. Abelard, "Letter to a Friend," p. 33.
5. Ibid., p. 64.
6. Ibid., p. 41.
7. Ibid.
8. Ibid., p. 42.
9. Heloïse, Preface to the *Lettres*, p. 18.
10. The couple had a son they named Astrolabe. Though he is mentioned in many sources as their newborn child, there is no mention of him afterwards, except to say that he was given over to the care of Abelard's family. Much later, near the end of her life, Heloïse mentions him when she asks a Church official to find him a good position. Although Abelard and Heloïse might be found guilty of child neglect today, at the time such an attitude was not uncommon. Neither was imbued with the parent archetype.
11. Heloïse, quoted by Abelard in "Letter to a Friend," p. 49.
12. Heloïse, quoted by Abelard in ibid., p. 54.
13. Heloïse, "Letters of Direction," p. 181.
14. Abelard, "Letter to a Friend," p. 58.
15. *Ency. Brit.*, Macropedia, vol. I, p. 11.
16. James Hillman, "Schism," p. 96.

Chapter 3

1. Abelard, "Love Letters," p. 117.
2. Ibid., p. 160.
3. Heloïse, "Love Letters," pp. 103–16.
4. Del McNeely, *Animus Aeternus*, p. 78.
5. Ibid.
6. Abelard, "Letter to a Friend," p. 46.
7. Preface, *Lettres D'Heloïse et D'Abelard*, p. 23.
8. Abelard, "Letters of Direction," p. 165.

9. Heloïse, "Love Letters," p. 110.
10. Preface, *Lettres D'Heloïse et D'Abelard*.

Chapter 4

1. Hillman, "Schism," p. 90.
2. *Webster's Third International Dictionary*, vol. III, p. 2371.
3. *Ency. Brit.*, Macropedia, vol. I, pp. 10–11.
4. Abelard, "Letters of Direction," pp. 161–62.

Chapter 5

1. Henri F. Ellenberger, *Discovery of the Unconscious*, p. 448.
2. Ibid., p. 450.
3. Guy Sorman, *Les Vrais Penseurs de Notre Temps*, p. 17.

Chapter 6

1. Jean Duvignaud, *The Genesis of the Passions in Social Life*, p. 36. The translations from the French are mine.
2. Ibid.
3. Hart, *Damage*, p. 34.
4. *Ency. Brit.*, Micropedia, vol. IX, p. 756.
5. Hart, *Damage*, p. 208.
6. Francesco Alberoni, *The In-Love Shock*, p. 56.

Chapter 7

1. Duvignaud, *The Genesis of the Passions*, p. 36.

Chapter 8

1. C. G. Jung, quoted in *Critical Dictionary of Jungian Analysis*, p. 82.
2. Milo Kundera, *Immortality*, pp. 232–36.
3. Hart, *Damage*, pp. 29–30.
4. Ibid., p. 46.
5. Ibid., p. 63.
6. Film, *Les Noces Blanches*.
7. Weil and Rosen, *Chocolate to Morphine*, p. 15.

Chapter 9

1. Adolf Guggenbühl-Craig, "The Demonic Side of Sexuality," p. 97.
2. Jane Urquhart, *Changing Heaven*, p. 97.
3. Ibid., p. 104.
4. Ibid., p. 110.
5. Ibid., p. 95.
6. Ibid., p. 98.
7. Ibid., p. 100.

Chapter 10

1. Hillman, "Schism," p. 83.

Chapter 11

1. Barbara Sullivan, *Therapy Grounded in the Feminine Principle*, p. 66.
2. Alice Miller, *The Drama of the Gifted Child*, pp. 9–12.
3. Sullivan, *Therapy Grounded*, p. 82.
4. Aldo Carotenuto, *Eros and Pathos*, p. 78.

5. Alberoni, *The In-Love Shock*, p. 71.
6. Ibid., p. 81.

Chapter 13

1. Robert Stein, *Incest and Human Love*, p. 148.
2. Ibid.
3. James Hillman, *The Myth of Analysis*, p. 98.
4. Jung, quoted in *Critical Dictionary of Jungian Analysis*, p. 138.
5. Margarete Mitscherlich, *La Femme Pacifique*, p. 44.
6. Hillman, *The Myth of Analysis*, p. 100.

Chapter 14

1. Jean Markale, *L'Amour Courtois ou le Couple Infernal*, pp. 87–89.
2. Ibid.
3. James Hillman, "Pothos," p. 60.
4. Ibid.
5. John Layard, *The Virgin Archetype*, p. 264.
6. Hillman, "Pothos," p. 54.

Bibliography

Alberoni, Francesco. *The In-Love Shock* (*Le Choc Amoureux*). Paris: Editions Ramsay, 1981.

Campbell, Joseph. *The Masks of the Gods: Creative Mythology.* New York: Penguin Books, 1968.

Carotenuto, Aldo. *Eros and Pathos.* Toronto: Inner City Books, 1989.

Duvignaud, Jean. *The Genesis of the Passions in Social Life* (*La Genèse des Passions dans la Vie Sociale*). Paris: Presses Universitaires de France, 1990.

Ellenberger, Henri F. *The Discovery of the Unconscious.* New York: Basic Books, Inc., 1970.

Encyclopedia Britannica, 15th ed.
Macropedia, volume I
Micropedia, volume IV
Micropedia, volume IX
Chicago: Encyclopedia Britannica Inc., University of Chicago, 1981.

Guggenbühl-Craig, Adolf. "The Demonic Side of Sexuality." In *Meeting the Shadow*, edited by Zweig and Adams. Los Angeles: Jeremy P. Tarcher, 1990.

Hart, Josephine. *Damage.* London: Chatto and Windus, 1991.

Hillman, James. *The Myth of Analysis: Three Essays in Analyti-*

cal Psychology. Evanston: Northwestern University Press, 1972.

_____. "Pothos: The Nostalgia of the Puer Eternus," 1979. "Schism as Differing Visions," 1974. Both articles published in *Loose Ends.* Dallas: Spring Publications, 1974.

Kundera, Milo. *Immortality (L'Immortalité).* Paris: Gallimard, 1990.

Layard, John. *The Virgin Archetype.* Zürich: Spring Publications, 1972.

Lettres D'Heloïse et D'Abelard. Geneva: La Guilde du Livre et Clairefontaine, 1970. These letters include the "Love Letters" between Heloïse and Abelard and the "Letters of Direction" they exchanged, as well as the "Letter to a Friend or Story of My Calamities" by Abelard.

Markale, Jean. *L'Amour Courtois ou le Couple Infernal.* Paris: Editions Imago, 1987.

McNeely, Del. *Animus Aeternus: Exploring the Inner Masculine.* Toronto: Inner City Books, 1991.

Miller, Alice. *The Drama of the Gifted Child.* New York: Basic Books, 1981.

Mitscherlich, Margarete. *La Femme Pacifique: Etude Psychoanalytique de l'Agressivité Selon le Sexe.* Paris: Des Femmes, 1988.

Samuels, Andrew; Shorter, Bani; and Plaut, Fred. *A Critical Dictionary of Jungian Analysis.* London: Routledge and Kegan Paul, 1986.

Sorman, Guy. *Les Vrais Penseurs de Notre Temps.* Paris: Librairie Arthème Fayard, 1989.

Stein, Robert. *Incest and Human Love.* Dallas: Spring Publications, 1973.

Sullivan, Barbara. *Therapy Grounded in the Feminine Principle.* Wilmette, Ill: Chiron Publications, 1990.

Urquhart, Jane. *Changing Heaven*. Toronto: McClelland and Stewart, 1990.

Webster's Third International Dictionary, vol. III. G. C. Merriam Co., 1976.

Weil, Andrew, and Rosen, Winifred. *Chocolate to Morphine*. Boston: Houghton Mifflin Co., 1983.

Lightning Source UK Ltd.
Milton Keynes UK
UKHW020254061222
413434UK00010B/828